Critical Guides to Spanish Texts

EDITED BY J.E. VAREY AND A.D. DEYERMOND

RIVERA

La vorágine

J. Walker

Professor of Spanish
Queen's University
Kingston, Ontario

Grant & Cutler Ltd *in association with*
Tamesis Books Ltd 1988

© Grant & Cutler Ltd
1988
ISBN 0 7293 0281 4

CC

I.S.B.N. 84-599-2307-X
DEPOSITO LEGAL: V. 482 - 1988

Printed in Spain by
Artes Gráficas Soler, S.A., Valencia
for
GRANT & CUTLER LTD
55-57, GREAT MARLBOROUGH STREET, LONDON W1V 2AY
and
27, SOUTH MAIN STREET, WOLFEBORO, NH 03894-2069, USA

Contents

To Irene

Prefatory Note

All references to *La vorágine*, which are taken from the Losada 9th edition (Buenos Aires, 1967), are incorporated in the body of the text by means of page numbers in parentheses. Italic figures given in parentheses, followed by page numbers, refer to the numbered entries in the Bibliographical Note.

To avoid excessive italicization of Spanish expressions I have left in their original form several words (for example, selva, cauchero, visitador, conquistador, etc.) which I consider common enough in this context to be acceptable in English usage.

I am grateful to the School of Graduate Studies and Research, Queen's University, for providing the research award which enabled me to prepare this manuscript; to Eleanor Smith and Paulette Bark who typed it; and to my wife Irene for her careful reading of typescript and proofs.

Introduction

One of the salient features of the treatment of the new novel (pre-boom, boom, and even post-boom) in Latin America has been the dismissive, if not downright hostile and contemptuous, attitude towards the traditional novel published in the first four decades of the twentieth century. Novels of the Mexican Revolution like *Los de abajo* (1916), the novel of the land, like *La vorágine* (1924), *Don Segundo Sombra* (1926), *Doña Bárbara* (1929), and the *indigenista* novel like *Huasipungo* (1934) have been wrapped in an all-embracing, pejorative blanket, ticketed 'traditional', to be regarded merely as quaintly interesting, as geographical/historical textbooks, or documents of social denunciation.[1]

The main criticism of these traditional novels is an alleged tendency to reflect, even to repeat, the characteristics of nineteenth-century fiction, as manifested in the Romantic-Realistic attitude towards the land, Americanism, and a creole realism which was to reach its peak in a kind of Zolaesque naturalism. It was José Eustasio Rivera's fate — a Romantic expression that he might have used and enjoyed — to have been born (in 1888) at that vital period in Latin American literature and history when the Modernist masters, in an effort to escape the harsh reality of a dehumanized industrial and political life, were not only beginning to display a conscious concern for art (under especially the influence of Symbolist and Parnassian models from France), but were also, in the face of the prevailing pessimistic views of the German philosophers Schopenhauer and Nietzsche, reflecting a change in their vital sensibility, which was, however, still very much rooted in the Romantic malaise — and paradoxically, in

---

[1] In his article 'El rasgo predominante en la novela hispanoamericana', in *La novela iberoamericana* (Albuquerque: University of New Mexico Press, 1952), José Antonio Portuondo describes the situation thus: 'Grave consecuencia del sentido instrumental, pragmático, dominante ... en la mayor parte de las novelas hispanomericanas, es que la crítica se ha acostumbrado a tratarlas como documentos y no como obras de arte, desdeñando lo estético para destacar sólo lo sociológico en ellas' (pp. 84-85).

Romantic idealism. In other words, Rivera is an aesthetic and philosophical product of his age. He could not be otherwise. To accuse him of reflecting to a certain degree the nineteenth-century values (literary and metaphysical) of Romanticism and Modernism is to denounce him for being a man of his time. Rivera died in 1928, even before the publication of *Doña Bárbara*, not to mention the *indigenista* novels of social protest of the 1930s, many of whose socio-economic-political characteristics he had prefigured in his searing indictment of the exploitation of the downtrodden rubber-workers and the Indians of the Colombian selva.

If *La vorágine* is a novel of the land, in which nature seems to be a protagonist, as early critics would have it, Rivera fits into a long line of Latin-American writers from the conquest onwards who have been fascinated and influenced by the wonders of the native soil. However, to brand *La vorágine* as merely a regionalist novel of social protest (which it undoubtedly is, at certain levels) is to underestimate the artistic quality of Rivera's work — important though the costumbrist and socio-political elements were in the 1920s, given the sociological and economic concerns of that time. For its other generally recognized praiseworthy quality, the psychological, *La vorágine* has received over the years at least limited praise for the portrayal of the unbalanced protagonist-narrator, Arturo Cova, whose psychological evolution has been compared to that of other creations by foreign masters like Conrad, Kafka and Dostoevsky — proof enough for the sceptics who seek to find the 'universal' label only outside Latin America.

But surely it is this capacity to transcend the national plane which will raise *La vorágine*, or any novel, above the mere regional work of art, or the mere social document, valuable and relevant as these aspects may be, in that area, at that time. It was mainly for these qualities that *La vorágine* received due praise in Colombia and the rest of Latin America on its publication in 1924. With the growing awareness of the psychological or analytical elements of the novel, as we shall see in Chapter 3, one begins to detect the existence of other elements to be appreciated at an even higher level which is super- or extra-American — that is, dare one say it, the universal.

With the emergence of the new novel and the new schools of criticism, scholars are now turning with fresh perspectives and modern tools of research to an even greater awareness of the hidden values of the previously underestimated, even derided, novels like *La vorágine*, in their search for what Carlos Fuentes calls the primal roots of all literary expression, i.e. poetry and myth, a dimension to be treated in Chapter 4. As a few scholars have begun to recognize, Rivera was already using myths and archetypes in *La vorágine* long before the advocates of the new narrative had sounded the clarion call. So too in his search for ideals and values (cf. Chapter 5) on the personal, national and universal planes, manifested through a poetic use of symbol and metaphor, Rivera was expressing his desire, and his ability, to lift the novel out of the jungles and plains of Colombia to a higher sphere, visible to, and appreciated by, all men. As is evidenced in Chapter 6, he was able to achieve all this through a demonstrable concern for the external aspects of art (form, narrative, structure, etc.) — a strong rejoinder to those critics who have long criticized *La vorágine* for its lack of form, jumbled narrative, chaotic structure, etc.

As Borges might have put it, there can be no new novel without its traditional predecessor. In these days of the post-boom one seeks to reappraise the old in the light of the new. There is no doubt that in the face of innovative ideas on literary theory, narratology, psychology, mythology, etc., novels like *Los de abajo*, *El hermano asno*, *Don Segundo Sombra* and *Doña Bárbara* are being read in a new way, revalued, and often rehabilitated through a basic kind of intertextuality. In Chapter 4, for example, I suggest that we can reread and re-evaluate *La vorágine* in the light of our familiarity with other classical treks or journeys, in Dante's *Divine Comedy*, Virgil's *Aeneid*, and Homer's *Odyssey* — as Rivera might have expected us to do. It is surely this constant searching for a re-examining of truth that keeps literature alive, dynamic and continually evolving for succeeding generations.

In this spirit of inquiry and open-mindedness we look again at *La vorágine*, once regarded as an important novel, but for limited reasons. To demonstrate that, like all great art, it can be read at, and does operate at, various levels, I intend to dismantle it, as it were, to highlight its various dimensions or planes — regionalist-nature, social protest, psychological, mythological-archetypal, search for values and ideals — then reconstruct it by linking the parts and putting them all together again. In so doing, and also by re-examining the format, the narrative, the structure, etc., one can appreciate better how Rivera has crafted all of this, and how he has woven the various threads into one strand. In the end, of course, it is only through the perfect fusion of this *forma* with the significant *fondo* that the great writer achieves the truly authentic work of art.

1 *Novel of the Land*

Although one should not simplify or generalize a complex literary and cultural process, the 1920s saw a rebirth of Americanism, in fictional terms represented by the three great classics of the American soil, *La vorágine* (1924) about the Colombian selva, Ricardo Güiraldes' *Don Segundo Sombra* (1926) about the Argentine pampa, and Rómulo Gallegos' *Doña Bárbara* (1929) about the Venezuelan llanura. That Rivera's novel should be the first of this genre places it in a unique position. To imply, however, that Rivera, who began his career under the influence of the Modernists, had totally rejected the European models, aesthetically or philosophically, in order to write 'la novela terrígena', is a grave distortion of the truth, as I shall demonstrate later.

There is no doubt that *La vorágine*, whatever its nomenclature, is one of the most powerful novels of the land written in Latin America. Rivera knew intimately the land that he describes in *La vorágine*. He had visited the llanos and the selva several times, as an inspector of petroleum deposits and as a member of a commission involved in the solution of border disputes between Colombia and Venezuela. In this capacity he met the Indians, suffered disease and illness, and knew first-hand the plain and especially the jungle, which was to have a dominant role to play in *La vorágine*. This selva was almost a character, perhaps even the protagonist, according to the limited and limiting theories of some critics which prevailed in the 1940s. In a sense, then, on this level the novel is about the struggle between man and nature (in nineteenth-century terms of civilization and barbarism).

Arturo Cova, the protagonist of *La vorágine*, as a city-dweller from Bogotá, is the civilized type who impetuously takes himself off to the jungle, for reasons which on the surface appear none too convincing. In Chapter 5, in my treatment of the search for values and ideals, I shall deal with Cova's motivation — apart from the obvious social reasons, because of which he wishes to escape from the clutches of interfering parents and a disapproving society in general. It is also appropriate that Cova is a poet in that he is going to be the narrator of this confrontation with the jungle. Alicia, his runaway mate, is less important at this stage as a woman than as a type, or a manifestation of Cova's search for ideal love, or as a vehicle for the fulfilment of at least one other of his vital values, paternity. The fact that the narrator-protagonist is also of unbalanced mind, and becomes increasingly so in his growing dealings with the jungle, highlights the psychological elements of the novel (see Chapter 3) and emphasizes my point about the overlapping of the various dimensions of the novel, and justifies the treatment and composition of this study.

It is no coincidence that the further the couple enters the jungle (and away from the civilized city), the less sympathetic and attractive nature becomes.[2] In the early pages of the novel, however, nature is still capable of being beautified and described in almost Modernist terms, in what is perhaps one of the set-pieces of natural description that Rivera was supposed to have composed on one of his earlier visits. The poet Cova is still close enough to the innocence and light of Bogotá to describe the dawn scene thus:

Y la aurora surgió ante nosotros: sin que advirtiéramos en el momento preciso, empezó a flotar sobre los pajonales un vapor sonrosado que ondulaba en la atmósfera como ligera muselina. Las estrellas se adormecieron, y en la lontananza de ópalo, al nivel de la tierra, apareció un celaje de incendio, una pincelada violenta, un coágulo de rubí. Bajo la gloria del alba hendieron el aire los patos chillones, las garzas morosas como copas flotantes, los loros esmeraldinos de tembloroso vuelo, las guacamayas multicolores. Y de todas partes, del pajonal y del espacio, del estero y de la palmera, nacía un hálito jubiloso que era vida, era acento, claridad y palpitación. Mientras tanto, en el arrebol que abría su palio inconmensurable, dardeó el primer destello solar, y lentamente, el astro, inmenso como una cúpula, ante el asombro del toro y la fiera, rodó por las llanuras

---

[2]In Chapter 5 I shall deal with another view of Bogotá as the centre of philistinism and the epitome of all that is false, evil and hypocritical, thus underlining the ambivalent attitude to the city that prevails in Cova's (and Rivera's) writings.

enrojeciéndose antes de ascender al azul. (20)

This is a beautifully artistic piece of work, close to the skilfully crafted sonnets of Rivera's collection, *Tierra de promisión* (1921).

If, however, the novel represents a struggle between man and nature, there is no doubt that by the end of Part 1 the lines are drawn, with nature being depicted in almost human terms as a terrible enemy (81). This changing conduct of nature has a corresponding effect on the psychological evolution of the protagonist, as we shall see in Chapter 3. By the beginning of Part 2 of the novel, in the powerful apostrophe to the selva, the altered state of nature, of Cova, and of Cova's mind, is frighteningly clear. This long passage, of which only parts can be quoted here, is strikingly powerful:

> — ¡Ah, selva, esposa del silencio, madre de la soledad y de la neblina! ¿Qué hado maligno me dejó prisionero en tu cárcel verde? ... ¡Tú me robaste el ensueño del horizonte y sólo tienes para mis ojos la monotonía de tu cenit ... !
>
> Tú eres la catedral de la pesadumbre ... Tú tienes la adustez de la fuerza cósmica y encarnas un misterio de la creación ... Déjame huir, oh selva, de tus enfermizas penumbras, formadas con el hálito de los seres que agonizaron en el abandono de tu majestad. Tú misma pareces un cementerio enorme donde te pudres y resucitas ... ¡Déjame tornar a la tierra de donde vine ... ! (95-96)

It is obvious, then, that by the beginning of Part 2 Cova's relations with the jungle are far from friendly.

As the novel progresses, and Cova's lack of mental balance increases, the jungle seems increasingly, in Cova's eyes, to become a person, especially in this Part 2 where the element of social exploitation (to be treated in Chapter 2) predominates. In their greed for rubber the workers attack the trees, and the selva, naturally, strikes back to defend itself: ' ... y mientras el cauchero sangra los árboles, las sanguijuelas lo sangran a él. La selva se defiende de sus verdugos, y al fin el hombre resulta vencido ... ' (135). Already in this opening chapter there is a link between nature and the mind of the protagonist, i.e. between the novel of the land and the psychological novel (as I shall demonstrate in Chapter 3). The man/jungle confrontation, as Cova portrays it, has a mutual effect. If the jungle destroys man, it is in revenge for the treatment meted out to the trees by the exploiting (and exploited) caucheros — which point immediately sends the mind jumping ahead to the abuses of jungle slavery (the theme of my Chapter 2 on the novel of social protest) (175). We have certainly come a long way from the beautiful Romantic verse of Rivera's *Tierra de promisión* — and from the Modernist praise of the exotic beauties of nature described in the opening pages of the novel, as Cova himself is astute enough to recognize:

¡Nada de risueñores enamorados, nada de jardín versallesco, nada de panoramas sentimentales! Aquí, los responsos de sapos hidrópicos, las malezas de cerros misántropos, los rebalses de caños podridos. Aquí, la parásita afrodisíaca que llena el suelo de abejas muertas; la diversidad de flores inmundas que se contraen con sexuales palpitaciones y su olor pegajoso emborracha como una droga; la *pringamosa* que inflama la piel, la pepa del *curujú* que parece irisado globo y sólo contiene ceniza cáustica, la uva purgante, el carozo amargo. (176)

If Rivera's critics needed proof that the poet had abandoned the world of regional costumbrismo or Modernist 'art for art's sake' poetry, there is ample evidence here in this passage of powerful description matching the powerful emotions he was trying to convey.

It is no wonder that Cova is afraid to provoke these inhuman, inimical trees, servants of 'la Diosa insaciable', for the selva imprisons men, swallows them, and annihilates them after attracting them into its embrace. Despite Cova's various roles as poet, dreamer, avenger, and social redeemer, there is no doubt that in the classic struggle between man and nature (an indifferent, cruel, sadistic nature), civilized man emerges, if he escapes at all, indelibly, irremediably marked and disfigured, a victim of the relentlessness of the jungle. In Cova's case, despite his heroic efforts, the end of his epic odyssey is clear, concise and final. His fate and that of his entourage is spelled out with brief and harrowing finality, in the last words of the novel: '¡Los devoró la selva!' (250).

Rivera's Treatment of Nature

The most cursory reading of Rivera's biography would indicate clearly that one of the sources of comfort for the young man, apart from a strong dependence on family (especially his mother), was the countryside of his native Colombia (Neiva and San Mateo) which always provided a refuge from the little tragedies of school and the failures of his youth. For many years he lived on a small hacienda, La Esmeralda, in the little town of San Mateo in Huila, where he worked the land and admired the countryside. These youthful experiences were to provide the inspiration and the material for his collection of sonnets, *Tierra de promisión*. His use of natural images and ambivalent metaphors relating to the sun and birds, especially the eagle, is an indication of his Romantic sensibility refined through the lens of art. In a sonnet like 'Soy un grávido río . . . ' his Romantic subjectivity is scarcely disguised, and it is only through a study, not only of the external elements of nature, but of the Romantic search for ideals (Chapter 5), which runs in a direct line from *Tierra de promisión* to *La vorágine*, that one can demonstrate the evolution of Rivera's view of nature depicted through Romantic symbols — and, one must add, with the Modernist's concern for the formal aspects of art (metre, style, rhythm).

Jean Franco (*11*) has clearly shown the importance of the natural surroundings of *La vorágine* as symbols of the protagonist's 'visión de la vida', as well as Rivera's skill in describing in convincing fashion Cova's 'trayectoria' — a word which seems to indicate the Romantic hero's inability to control his own fate. It is no coincidence that in Part 1 of the novel, as Cova leaves the city for the open plain, one sees a change in his and Rivera's attitude to nature. The hardships encountered on the 1922 journey to the selva on border-dispute business confirmed for Rivera that this nature was not the same that had provided the solace of his youth. It is no surprise, then, that the publication of *La vorágine* two years later should give a different picture of nature from that described in the sonnets. This is now a cruel, malevolent nature that reflects more accurately the prevailing pessimism and *angustia* of Rivera. Arturo Cova reflects, of course, something of this evolution in the author's character.

While he is on the plain, symbol of infinity and eternity, there is still opportunity for the spirit to free itself from earthly limitations, as Jean Franco points out (*11*, p. 104). The further he enters into the jungle and leaves the plain behind, the spiritual flights become rarer, until eventually, once entrapped in the selva, there is no liberty possible. If the plain is characterized by water, at the end of Part 1, through the sacrificial and destructive force of fire, Cova reaches a demonic, infernal state: '¿Qué había logrado mi perseverancia contra la suerte? ¡Dios me desamparaba y el amor huía! . . . ¡En medio de las llamas empecé a reír como Satanás!' (94). The classic symptoms and typical terminology of the doomed Romantic hero are not lost on the attentive reader.

By the beginning of Part 2 Cova is truly a prisoner in the green hell of the jungle: '¿Qué hado maligno me dejó prisionero en tu cárcel verde?' (95) — from which he begs to be freed in the powerful apostrophe to the jungle already quoted. In this sense his prisoner status echoes the fate of other exemplary Romantic heroes. The description of the green hell-prison and Cova's situation therein are a long way from the happier moments of the plain which Cova remembers in a 'nébula dulce', with nature depicted in Modernist terms of prose poetry — 'crepúsculos cariñosos', 'cielo amigo', with palm trees weeping and waving in sympathy with the now lost travellers. But these scenes exist only in memory. The Modernist dream is but that — a dream, an illusion, an artificial creation: '¿Cuál es aquí la poesía de los retiros, donde están las mariposas que parecen flores translúcidas, los pájaros mágicos, el arroyo cantor? ¡Pobre fantasía de los poetas que sólo conocen las soledades domesticadas!' (176). Reality is the croaking of dropsical toads, the undergrowth traps of treacherous mounds, and scum-covered ponds full of rotting tree trunks. Cova, like the younger Rivera of the sonnets, had in better times viewed nature in these terms: 'Quizá mi fuente de poesía estaba en el secreto de los bosques intactos, en la caricia de las auras, en el idioma desconocido de las cosas; en cantar lo que dice al peñón la onda que se despide, el arrebol a la ciénaga, la estrella a las inmensidades que guardan el silencio de Dios' (74-75). What the poet of the jungle now sees is a nightmare world of deformed trees, blind reptiles, man-eating ants, obscene plants, poisonous flowers, malignant undergrowth, etc. As William Bull states with brutal frankness: 'The Amazon forest, whose many natural beauties have been delightfully

and *objectively* described by both laymen and scientists, becomes a
seething, writhing, tortured mass of disgusting life struggling in a
kind of botanical warfare and tainted by "el hálito del fermento, los
vapores calientes de la penumbra, el sopor de la muerte, el marasmo
de la procreación" ' (*3*, p. 313, my italics). I have emphasized the
word 'objectively' since the basis of Bull's criticism of Cova's description of nature is hardly fair: the natural picture painted is the
product of a deranged mind who happens to be an artist, and who
will, therefore, poeticize the malevolent nature of the selva, just as
earlier he had depicted the beauties of the plain in Modernist terms.
If this prettifying of nature in Part 1 is bad poetics and represents by
Bull's reasoning the pathetic fallacy, what are we to make of Cova's
later descriptions of the selva? Is this 'furious realism' portrayed by
Cova to be considered as 'objective reality' or distorted and exaggerated, that is, telluric naturalism? Is it realistic, or only a realistic
manifestation of the state of Cova's unbalanced mind? Is a Kodak
type of reality superior to a Goya type of reality? Surely the latter,
the reflection of the disturbed protagonist's mind, is aesthetically
authentic and valid. A total reading of the novel, rather than exclus-
ive classifications of *La vorágine* as a novel of the land, or social
document, or psychological novel, clearly reinforces my point that
Cova's view of nature is coloured by his psychological evolution,
which is itself a product of the influence of this very nature – surely
one of the master touches by which Rivera has managed to synthesize the complete novel out of a series of different narratives.

Some critics have claimed that other characters like Clemente
Silva and Esteban Ramírez give more realistic pictures of nature than
Cova, and in this sense are more trustworthy narrators. But in Bull's
estimation, all three are routine types, unstable and incapable of distinguishing between illusion and reality; therefore one never gets an
objective view of nature throughout the novel. Bull seems to miss
the point that even if the other narrators were deemed to be more
balanced and therefore more objective in their description of the
jungle, the narratological reality (because of Rivera's structure of the
novel) is that all the stories of all the characters are filtered through
the mind of the protagonist and principal narrator, Cova, and recorded in literary terms through the artistic (albeit unbalanced) mind of
the poet-hero. (I shall treat the merits of this narrative mode at

length in Chapter 6.)

If Rivera did not consider his characters abnormal, and identified with them completely, then their interpretation is his. And if so, does this fact destroy the validity of the novel as social document, in its depiction of the conditions of the rubber-workers? — a key function of *La vorágine*, by Rivera's own admission, as I shall demonstrate in Chapter 2. In other words, does the untrustworthiness of the narrator have an influence on the efficacy of the novel as sociopolitical denunciation? If our function here were to examine *La vorágine* only from the perspective of a social document, one might quote modern critics (like Eyzaguirre) for whom the social aspect of the novel fails because of Clemente Silva's narrative and his final failure to locate Cova and his party (*8*, pp. 88-89). The irony is, as I shall demonstrate in Chapter 3, that although Cova's manuscript, including Silva's weighty story of social abuses, failed to move the government or the Colombian people of the time, Rivera's novel has survived as, amongst its several functions, a searing indictment of the exploitation of the rubber-workers, just as the author (pehaps misguidedly) would have wished.

But surely, as Franco has rightly pointed out, 'Plains, rivers, vortex, jungle are thus both real landscapes and aspects of human experience' (*11*, p. 109). As such, they transcend the purely regional, national, and, of course, natural level of the novel to reach universal heights in their depiction of the human condition, and men's dreams and ambitions (fulfilled or not) in their search for values in life, That one can go back at least one step to the familiar Romantic landscape to trace Arturo Cova's trajectory from city to plain to jungle, from civilization to barbarism, from freedom to captivity, from the liberty of life to 'la vórtice de la nada' reveals at least one dimension of the past which helps to raise the novel above the telluric pamphlet. In succeeding chapters, especially Chapter 4, I shall develop this thesis by suggesting that *La vorágine* goes back even further to Rennaissance and medieval sources, and eventually to mythological origins, in its depiction of the human condition, types and symbols.

Costumbrismo

Many scholars have studied *La vorágine, Don Segundo Sombra* and *Doña Bárbara* exclusively for their costumbrist elements. Although one recognizes the value of such research in any regional literature, it is a stage that one must pass through and transcend. If not, it may well stress the superficial or the local to the exclusion of the more profound and universal. Although one hopes that criticism on *La vorágine* has indeed crossed that threshold, there is no doubt that the novel is a mine of information about the life and customs of the rubber-workers, Indians, and other inhabitants of the plains and jungle of Colombia in the first decades of this century.

In terms of costumbrismo, the narrative of *La vorágine* is a fruitful source of data for scholars who wish to accompany and understand Cova and Alicia in their flight through the plains of Casanare, the affairs at Hato Grande (its real name), their stay at the Barracas del Guaracú, and finally their escape to the rubber regions of Yaguanarí, where they were eventually swallowed up by the selva. In the vast sweep of his novel Rivera has provided a veritable encyclopedia of customs, lists of plants, animals, trees, flowers, etc. His descriptions of the food, the diversions, the religious beliefs and superstitions of the forest- and plain-dwellers constitute a wealth of material fit to fill any history of Colombian culture. Apart from the normal, mundane details relating to eating, living arrangements, customs, entertainment and daily existence, useful to anthropologists, his contribution to folklore, philology and musicology is inestimable. Details about the various songs and dances like the *tonada* and the *llorao* are mingled with fascinating information about ballads, local sayings, proverbs and other words of popular wisdom (*20*, p. 320). In fact, *La vorágine* contains so many words peculiar to the region that Rivera had to provide a glossary to the novel.

Any careful reader must be indebted to Neale-Silva for his research into such esoteric matters as the superstitious practices of the Indians (*20*, p. 321) – for example, the mixing of the heart of the *piapoco* with coffee and the use of the aphrodisiac 'venga, venga', magical prayers and incantations, the special cure for fevers produced by certain leaves plucked from high up in the tree – those from the lower part make the patient vomit (41). The novel is replete with references to and stories of ghosts and fairies, witches (e.g. 61), and powerful Indian spirits, especially the Indiecita Mapiripama (120). One remembers Bull's pejorative description of the novel (as part of his attack on its lack of objective reality) as a 'hobgoblin forest straight out of an evil fairy tale' (*3*, p. 317). One can take this description not only as a product of Cova's deranged mind but of Rivera's extensive folkloric and anthropological research, and turn it into a compliment to the author's handling of the costumbrist element, which becomes, rather than just local colour, an integral part of the artistic and psychological totality of the novel.

Not unlike the gauchos of the pampas, or the vaqueros of the llanuras of Venezuela, the inhabitants of the Colombian plains are a formidable lot (forever close to danger and therefore unafraid of death), whose main sources of entertainment were primitive and crude, rooted in their strength, *hombría,* and thirst for blood — horse-taming (40-41), cockfights (70), the rodeo (85-86), and other manifestations of the never-ending struggle between civilization and barbarism, between man and nature, which usually ends in death (89). As elsewhere in Latin America, the Indian suffered great deprivation at the hands of the white exploiters, in this case the rubber magnates like Narciso Barrera, Funes, and El Cayeno. In *La vorágine* Rivera describes the life of the Guahivos (of fierce repute), the Piapocos, Cuivas, Sálivas and others, all of whom he had met on his travels.

Although the experiences of the llanos and the selva were centuries and worlds apart from his comfortable, consoling life in Neiva, Rivera, in *La vorágine*, is always an acute and sensitive observer of nature — both in its malevolent shape of destructive, debilitating, bloodsucking, maddening selva, and in its few benevolent descriptions of the beauty of the multi-coloured dawn scene or the high-soaring birds of the jungle flying, like Cova's ideals, far above the tormented turmoil of the vortex where only the fittest survive.

Survival is the keynote, in literature as in life. These costumbrist details by themselves are of little value if inserted in the novel for the mere effect of local colour. If *La vorágine* were only a handbook, a manual of regional or national interest, it would be useful enough, but would not transcend the mere nature study or travel book. The painting of customs, like the novel of the land of which it is part, does not exist for its own sake, nor should it. For Rivera, poet and artist, the natural descriptions are essential components of the aesthetic entity. Selva, plain, river and vortex are all part of the real face of nature in the novel, but they are also symbols of, and formative elements in, the human condition, the treatment of which in all its manifestations (natural, social, psychological) constitutes the raison d'être and the soul of *La vorágine*.

2 *Document of Social Protest*

La vorágine is, of course, much more than a dual struggle (man versus nature, man versus man), but Curcio (*6*, pp. 176-77) does well to link these two aspects of Rivera's novel. If one obvious component of Rivera's *colombianidad* is his preoccupation with the land, and a desire to paint its types, customs and the national *modo de ser*, another key aspect of his concern with things Colombian is his political awareness, his great sense of civic duty, and a patriotism which is inextricably bound up with the search for values, personal and national (as I shall demonstrate in Chapter 5). If Rivera's sense of patriotism seems overdeveloped, one must remember that his life (short as it was) ran parallel with a series of historical events which kept the socio-economic and political elements in the foreground of his, and the national, perspective – the loss of Panama, the War of the 1000 Days, the atrocities of the 1914-18 War, and the exhausting and fruitless border disputes with Venezuela and Peru.

As a Conservative representative, and as a member of various government commissions, Rivera was keenly aware of his duty as a Colombian, in particular with the endemic problem of frontier invasions and squabbles, and the subsequent abuses that emanated from the illegal occupations. But, with the failure of his voice in the Chamber of Representatives, it is no surprise that he should take up the pen, and that his literary efforts should gain the attention which he had failed to obtain by diplomatic and political measures. However, notwithstanding the emphasis of this chapter, one must underscore the fact that Rivera's apparent socio-political document is an artistic manifestation of his personal beliefs which he rendered in literary terms in *La vorágine*. Despite his oft-repeated, and often misguided, protestations about the authenticity of his novel – which are understandable given his reforming zeal – in quieter moments of reflection and illumination Rivera manages to put the politics/literature problem in perspective. When questioned once as to whether he was more interested in literature or in politics, he answered: 'La literatura, sin duda alguna. De la política no he sacado sino el conocimiento de los hombres, de sus miserias, que me suministrarán elementos para mi obra literaria futura en alguna forma' (*21*, p. 345).

In his concern, however, to stress the authenticity of his novel as a social document in order to make political profit — for the best possible motive, national well-being — Rivera occasionally exaggerated this aspect of his work to the point of indiscretion. For example, in his desire to highlight the novel as history or documentary evidence, he had several photographs included in an early edition to authenticate the socio-historical dimension — 'Arturo Cova, en las barracas de Guaracú — Fotografía tomada por la madona Zoraida Ayram'; plus one that purports to be 'El cauchero Clemente Silva'. In reply once to a questioner about the reality of *La vorágine*, Rivera replied: 'Casi en su totalidad. Yo vi todas esas cosas. Los personajes que allí figuran son todos entes vivos y aun algunos de ellos llevan sus nombres propios' (*21*, p. 305). Apart from the fact that it does a great disservice to the imaginative and creative faculties of the author, and to the artistic qualities of the novel, this statement is not completely true. Like most fiction, the novel was based on real events, living people (El Pipa, Barrera), and many of the horrors, such as the Putumayo killings, had been well documented by other writers (for example, Sir Roger Casement in his House of Commons report).[3] Rivera has depicted places and events with great accuracy, which can be verified by consulting other texts, for example, George Bisson's *Casanare* (Bogotá, 1896), occasionally changing the names of people and places. Julio César Arana, the rubber king of the Peruvian Amazon Company, did exist: see W.W. Hardenburg, *The Putumayo: The Devil's Paradise* (London, 1913). The French scientist Eugène Robuchon was almost certainly murdered in 1906 because he saw too much and, horrified by his experiences, sent photographs of the atrocities to Lima and Europe. Zoraida Ayram was Narcisa Saba, widow of Barrera Malo, owner of a hotel-type-house at Puerto Carreño in the jungle. Tomás Funes, responsible for the crimes of San Fernando, murdered the governor Roberto Pulido, and took his position. The visitador was probably a composite figure, like many

[3] 'Correspondence Respecting the Treatment of British Colonial Subjects and Native Indians in the Putumayo District, Including Sir Roger Casement's Report', *House of Commons Report* 68 (1912-13), Miscellaneous No. 8.

of *La vorágine*'s characters, and Clemente Silva was probably a par-
tial invention of Rivera, although there were many such guides in the
jungle on whom he could have based his character. In other words,
the factual basis of *La vorágine* has never been in dispute, but
Rivera, in his desire for authenticity, is wrong to suggest the total
reality of his novel — a claim which severely undercuts his artistic
reputation.

There can be no doubt, then, that *La vorágine* is a historical record and a social document, but Rivera and those who follow his example do his novel a disservice on those occasions when they stress
excessively the importance of the novel exclusively or especially as
an authentic portrayal of the reality of social abuses, and thus underline its denunciatory component, to the detriment of its other more
lasting qualities and deeper dimensions. These socio-political elements, the factual bases, and the biographical data of *La vorágine* are
not, however, incompatible with the universal dimension to which
any true work of art aspires. In his concern for the exploited, the
downtrodden and the oppressed, and motivated by his exalted patriotism, Rivera has at times overstressed this aspect of the novel,
causing those proponents of the social-document school to fall into
the trap described above. The important point about the novel, surely, is that it transcends the events, the episodes, and the characters
portrayed here, to attain what Neale-Silva calls 'una transrealidad
poética', without in any way weakening the other strain. The conscious artist and the conscientious writer, who continually rewrote
and revised his work, chose instead to take the aesthetic route, just-
ifying my contention that good literature can be propagandistic, but
propaganda can never be good literature.

Search for Social Justice in 'La vorágine'

As I have tried to demonstrate throughout this study, to stress un-
duly the novel of social protest, and to isolate it from the novel of
the land, or the psychological novel, or the search for values novel, is
to highlight the unidimensional in a multi-dimensional novel, and
thereby detract from the richness of the whole. But there is no
doubt that the socio-political element was, as we have seen, of such
great importance to Rivera that he was prepared to distort his artistic priorities at times in order to use the work of art as a political

weapon to convince an ignorant public and especially the uncaring politicians. This long-standing preoccupation is reflected in the attitude and the conduct of his creation, Arturo Cova, as revealed by the protagonist's narrative.

There is even less doubt that Part 2 of the novel, narrated by Clemente Silva and devoted to the horrible treatment of the rubberworkers in the Putumayo, is the most full and detailed description of the atrocities against which Cova (and Rivera) protested so vehemently. No less horrifying are the stories of Helí Mesa and Ramiro Estévanez in Parts 2 and 3, with regard to the maltreatment of both the peons and the Indians. Although the events of the novel take place in the space of seven months, Rivera, with artistic licence (despite his claims to authenticity), covers the first two decades of this century, culminating in the Funes massacre at San Fernando.

Although Parts 2 and 3 of the novel constitute the core and the culmination of the search for social justice, in a sense it is rooted in the character of Cova, who flees from Bogotá ostensibly because of his dissatisfaction with its social values and customs and with the bourgeois morality of Alicia's parents who want to marry her off to an older landowner. As early as the first pages of the novel at La Maporita, Rivera introduces the figure of Narciso Barrera, the epitome of selfishness and exploitation, and the symbolic obstacle to Cova's individual and collective sense of justice. Barrera's conduct — flirting with Alicia, corrupting the workers, cheating at cards — inflames Cova's jealousy and infuriates his sense of justice throughout Part 1, culminating in his desire to kill his enemy. Behind the personal animosity and hostility, therefore, is the criticism of the justice system 'que anda extraviada', and the conditions permitted by the government, which reach their peak (in Part 1) in the description of the corrupt judge, José Isabel Rincón Hernández, a friend of Barrera, whose abuses have gained him a notorious reputation in his circuit for soliciting bribes and imposing fines (79).

Thus it becomes clear early in the novel that if one tragic element is the classic man-versus-nature theme, the other no less horrifying theme is the man-versus-man struggle with wicked creatures perpetrating inhuman acts on the less fortunate, in a manner even more cruel than that of a telluric nature. In Part 1 Rivera prepares the way for this aspect of the novel, through his introduction of the charac-

ter of Barrera, the mere instrument of more powerful men like Funes. The portrait of the corrupt judge, the arm of the law, illustrates
in no uncertain manner that (as Rivera constantly proclaimed in the
Chamber of Representatives) the government was at least as much to
blame for not only permitting such flagrant abuses of the legal and
penal system, but condoning them in the name of law and order, to
the benefit of big business. By the end of Part 1, then, Cova, frustrated by the abuses of the justice system, and powerless to prevent
the everpresent corruption, makes the important link between the
unjust system and his personal emotions, when Alicia is abducted by
the personification of evil, Barrera.

Although Arturo Cova is the protagonist of the novel, and everything is seen through his eyes (including distant social abuses), in
Parts 2 and 3 of the novel, Rivera, to alter the tirade and perhaps to
add to the socio-political authenticity as well as the narrative variety,
has the protagonist meet other characters who relate their adventures. In this way the novel becomes a polyphonic chorus of prot-
ests, thus reinforcing the solitary cry of the protagonist, and strengthening Cova's (and Rivera's) claim to be relating the truth. In this
way Arturo Cova speaks for and to, as well as introducing, the different characters, like Helí Mesa, in the opening pages of Part 2; especially Clemente Silva, whose tragic, pathetic story and litany of abuses
take up all of Part 2 and some of Part 3; and Esteban Ramírez, the
witness to many of the evils perpetrated in Part 3.

Helí Mesa, an old friend of Fidel Franco, tells the brutal story of
how Barrera had made the hapless peons drunk, and had lured them
away, together with Fidel's wife (la niña Griselda) and Alicia, under
the pretence of a business expedition; Barrera then tried to justify
his behaviour by saying that they had strayed into Venezuelan terr-
itory. Helí Mesa's story of the plight of the poor women and children imprisoned in the boats and dying of thirst and sunstroke reaches its peak of naturalistic description in the harrowing version of the
death of one mother and child, which prompted his own escape,
whilst Barrera sailed off comfortably installed in another boat, ostensibly to wage a complaint against the chief villain, Colonel Funes
(116). (As I have tried to indicate throughout this study, it is a tribute to Rivera's skill as a total novelist that one has great difficulty in
isolating one strand of the novel from another. The child/mother

episode described above makes Cova think of Alicia and his future child, and the role of paternity (117), themes which I shall develop in Chapter 3 and especially in Chapter 5.)

But this episode is only a sample of what is normal practice in the ongoing wars between the various groups who are dedicated to the task of ravaging the rubber trees, killing the Indians, and any other poor souls who can no longer be exploited. Barrera is but an instrument in the hands of more powerful men like Funes and El Cayeno ('cauteloso y cruel como un cazador', 139). No story, however, is more tragic than that of old Clemente Silva, who had travelled the jungle for over sixteen years as a cauchero, and still does not possess a cent. Through the figure of Silva we have the most detailed picture of what happens to those slave-caucheros (and their offspring) not only at the hands of their exploiters, but also at the hands of the jungle which strikes back at its enemies (135). This man/nature/man reaction is another variation of the civilization/barbarism theme in the natural setting. The selva not only defends itself physically against the intruders, but also insidiously corrupts and vitiates their minds and bodies so that they too end up by destroying their colleagues in distress.

Nowhere is Don Clemente more eloquent than in his description of the poor souls (whites and Indians) who are voluntary or slave workers, serving monsters like El Cayeno, Colonel Funes, or the Turkish woman Zoraida Ayram, a Doña Bárbara-type man-eater, for whom Clemente had been a servant, bought as a slave to pay off his debts and later sold like a beast of burden to Pezil, another Turk, to work in the rubber *gomales* of Yaguanará (where Alicia had been taken by Barrera). Clemente Silva relates all this with a conviction and factual accuracy which can stem only from Rivera's own observations, investigations and strong feelings about the exploitation of his compatriots. By the flashback descriptions of the early years and the quest for his long-lost son (dead or alive), plus his experiences working for the company of the Peruvian Arana, who had promised women and pleasures to those who captured Indians for the rubber-gathering, Silva provides a panoramic view of the life and times of the exploited.

If Peruvians, Venezuelans, and other foreigners are often responsible for the crimes suffered by the workers, at least one sympathetic

foreigner is concerned enough to listen to Clemente Silva's complaints about the slave conditions — that is, the aforementioned
French *mosiú*, explorer and naturalist, a character based on the
French scientist, Eugène Robuchon, who was eliminated by the
criminal agents of the Putumayo. Having captured and immortalized
with his Kodak camera the condition of the scarred trees ('castrados
ambiguamente por los gomeros', 150) and the bloodied, lashed body
of Don Clemente, the French scientist seeks with notes, dossiers,
speeches and photographic evidence to convince the authorities in
London, Paris and Lima of the heinous crimes committed against the
workers in the name of progress and commerce. When he complains
to the company-owners, the scientist's fate is predictable.

What the French explorer was prevented from doing, the Colombian visitador (' . . . hombre enérgico . . . pero sin malicia ni observa-
ción', 158) is not capable of doing, because of the cover-up of the
abuses during the week of his trip, the fear of the workers to speak
out, and the inability of the Indians to understand their physical and
financial slavery. What chance do the exploited workers have, when
the real crime is, as Rivera states here and in Congress, committed
not in the selva but in Bogotá where the sell-out to Arana, named
honorary consul in Iquitos, takes place? Also, the president of the
republic allows General Velasco to license troops in the Putumayo
to protect the foreign colonizers of the Colombian river. In other
words, troops, money and authority are put at the disposal of foreigners to be used against the Colombian people. These problems,
which are matters of justice, national rights and pride, can be solved
only in Bogotá and Lima, as Rivera was wont to proclaim in the
Chamber of Representatives, in various reports, and in many articles
in the Colombian press.

Convinced by the eloquence and courage of his politically shrewd
companion, Balbino Jácome, who sees beyond the local level of
these evils, Clemente Silva plans to go to the Colombian consulate in
Manaos on the Río Negro to denounce the crimes of the chief exploiters, to reveal all his acquired information about the slave and
the French scientist, and to set the record straight once and for all
(164), as well as to find his lost son — no mean task. When the old
guide does find the representative of his country, the latter proves to
be neither Colombian nor interested in Colombia, and suggests that

Silva should pass his information on the missing scientist to the French consul. As Part 2 concludes with the failure of Clemente Silva's mission, Rivera, with an ironic but fitting ending (cf. the satanic incendiary climax of Part 1), has Clemente Silva receive the information that his son, according to one report, has been killed by a falling tree.[4] Nature, it appears, has struck back again, in a personal way. Yet once more the author displays his fine ability to synthesize his themes and pull all the strands together by linking the failure of Silva's personal mission (search for his son) with the national search (patriotism *manqué*), through this bitter indictment and brutal exposé of exploitation, maltreatment and social injustice, to which Rivera devoted his political life.

Although Clemente Silva's story is still not complete at the end of Part 2, most of it has unfolded. Although in Part 3 Don Clemente no longer narrates in the first person, the litany of abuses, personal and collective, suffered by the old man and his colleagues continues, but is now narrated by Cova who also adopts not only the cause but the the identity of the exploited worker. Part 3 begins thus: '¡Yo he sido cauchero, yo soy cauchero!' (169). With these words the hitherto implied social mission of Arturo Cova becomes explicit. Now the first person experiences of Clemente Silva are revealed, as it were, by Cova, who becomes a kind of channel for the complaints of the caucheros, and also their spokesman.

Escaping with some of his companions from the clutches of the Turk Fezil to whom he served as a guide, Clemente Silva survives the poisonous insects and the marching ants devouring everything in their path. Silva, who later finds the bones of his fleeing companions, wanders around like an animal for two months, with no fire and no gun for protection, until he is found by the Albuquerques from whom he flees by canoe to the Vaupés River in the never-ending search for his son's bones, only to be captured by El Cayeno, in whose service he was when Cova found him. Although the above-mentioned adventures and sufferings of the old guide are narrated through the protagonist, they are no less harrowing or immediate in their impact for having been told in the third person by Cova. In

---

[4] In fact, in Part 3, near the end of the novel, we discover that Lucianito shot himself in suspicious circumstances in the arms of la Madona — or so she relates his death to Cova.

fact, these events contribute greatly to the theme, and the verisimilitude, of the protagonist's conversion to social redeemer, seen as
they are through Cova's eyes.

The third main narrative voice in the depiction and denunciation
of social abuses is that of Esteban Ramírez. After Cova's own adventures with the sensuous, langorous la Madona (' ¡Mujer singular,
mujer ambiciosa, mujer varonil!' 199) and the blustering 'General'
Váquiro (El Cayeno's henchman), Cova meets his old friend Esteban
Ramírez from their youthful days in Bogotá, when he was known as
Ramiro Estévanez. Ramírez proves to be a fascinating mirror of
Cova's character, his alter ego, as it were, − an interesting psychological phenomenon which I shall develop in Chapter 3. He is now
blind, as a result of a burning-rubber accident, an affliction which is
a symbolic revenge for his having witnessed one of the most heinous
crimes ever committed by man on man, the massacre of San Fernando de Atabapo by Colonel Funes.

Although Funes was responsible for this particular massacre, the
point that Rivera is trying to make is that the colonel's act is only a
symptom of the real problem which is more deeply rooted in the
national *modo de ser*: 'Funes es un sistema, un estado de alma, es la
sed de oro, es la envidia sórdida. Muchos son Funes, aunque lleve
uno solo el nombre fatídico' (218). One notes again, as in the case of
the latter part of Clemente Silva's adventures, that Cova narrates the
events as they had been told to him by Esteban Ramírez. Cova becomes a kind of filter for the events which thus emerge as the product of his now highly developed sense of social mission − not to
mention his jungle-influenced mind, and his poetic sensibility. But
the results could not be otherwise, since the system permits, encour-
ages, facilitates such conduct. Thus the very way of life is based on
fraud and corruption, both individual and corporate, not to mention
governmental. There can be no justice because the judge is too busy
supplying the governor with mañoco. As Rivera succinctly and ironically summarizes the situation: 'Esto allí es legal, correcto y humano' (219).

Faced with such overwhelming evidence, through the narratives
of Helí Mesa, Clemente Silva, Balbino Jácome and Esteban Ramírez,
Cova finally recognizes what Silva had found throughout his experiences, that even is he does manage to deliver the letter to the

Colombian consul in Manaos, the latter will surely absolve himself of any responsibility by intimating that his jurisdiction does not extend to such latitudes; or worse still, since he is not a Colombian, that his word prevails only in his own area; or, having scrutinized carefully the map of Colombia, will claim that since such rivers do not appear thereon, they must belong to Venezuela to whose consul proper representations should be made. And the consul will continue to remain entrenched in his ignorance, because poor Colombia is not known or recognized by its own sons – or by its cartographers and geographers.

The many references to nationality and patriotism are not a coincidence in Rivera's plea for social and civic justice. As his career shows, the plight of those caught in the throes of frontier disputes with Brazil, Venezuela and Peru (personal level) as well as the political implications of the disputes themselves (national level), were his major concern as a politician. The fact that he was involved in the investigation and the legal wrangling to settle these disputes – in favour of Colombia, of course – gives an authentic ring to the descriptions, and a strength to the conviction of his patriotism and sense of *colombianidad*, one of his life-giving ideals, as I shall demonstrate in Chapter 5. Rivera's attempts to transcend the purely personal in all of his descriptions of the abuses and to raise the problem to the national level, legally and civically, are seen in the important role that Cova attributes to the Colombian consul. Although Clemente Silva is disillusioned with his attempts to find help at the consulate, Cova nonetheless reiterates his patriotic faith in the desire and the capacity of the consul to come to the aid of the oppressed – on receipt of Cova's letter of advocacy to be delivered by the peripatetic herald of misfortune, Clemente Silva. When Cova leaves the letter for the consul in Santa Iasbel, it is to invoke from the consul not help for himself but ' . . . sus sentimientos humanitarios en alivio de mis compatriotas, víctimas del pillaje y la esclavitud, que gimen entre la selva, lejos de hogar y patria, mezclando al jugo de caucho su propia sangre' (246). When Cova kills Barrera, he no longer rejoices in merely having rid himself of a personal enemy, the abductor of his ideal woman. His words take on a higher meaning, a patriotic tone: 'Ya libré a mi patria del hijo infame. Ya no existe el enganchador' (247). It is no wonder that by the last page of the novel, he, who had started out on an impulsive personal adventure, is now regarded by his companions in distress as a kind of messianic figure or social redeemer.[5]

Moreover, having recorded in writing all these experiences, Arturo Cova also becomes the apologist-historian of the rubber-workers and their abuses, by entrusting the notebook (which becomes the manuscript of the novel, as we shall see in Chapter 6) to, appropriately, the character who epitomizes the sufferings of the workers, Clemente Silva. It was the old guide's sacred duty to hand it over to the consul so that the true history of the various episodes, symptomatic of the general national malaise, might be told and preserved forever, as a message and a warning to all Colombians: 'Cuide mucho esos manuscritos y póngalos en manos del cónsul; son la historia nuestra, la desolada historia de los caucheros' (249). If it does not tell the whole story, Cova's manuscript (and Rivera's novel) at least serves as a warning and a bitter indictment of a national evil, an important socio-economic-political document, and a call to patriotism which some Colombians were to take up in their defence of human rights and national concern for those marginal sections of society (Indians, poor, day-workers) in distant parts of the country far from Bogotá.

That Rivera felt obliged to investigate such abuses is to his credit. That he should have written a novel to reveal his discoveries and bring his findings before the scrutiny of the nation is doubly meritorious – and, for some, motive enough for writing *La vorágine*. Despite the express social intention of Rivera, *La vorágine* transcends the mere document of denunciation, as it does the novel of the land, through its subtle and analytical portrayal of man and his psyche – one man in particular, the protagonist Arturo Cova, a complex being whose psychological development goes far beyond the mere relating of adventures, personal and national, rising to universal heights in its analysis of the human mind.

---

[5] In Chapter 5, in my treatment of Cova's search for ideals, I shall argue that, in a sense, at the very end of the novel, Cova, by turning his back on the lepers, rejects the social-redeemer label to protect his wife and child, thus making a personal choice for something less lofty, something more human.

3 *Psychological Case History*

In his well-known *Historia de la literatura hispanoamericana* (Mexico City: Fondo de Cultura Económica, 1961), Enrique Anderson Imbert affirms that *La vorágine* is important for two reasons – as a novel of social protest and for its interesting psychological development (II, p. 90). It is, of course, much more, as I have tried to suggest, but Anderson Imbert's brief, pertinent, though incomplete summary reinforces the link between this chapter and the preceding one. In fact, I should like to propose that this chapter on the psychological development of the protagonist is a key section of this study and is central to the other chapters, both preceding and succeeding, which depend on and revolve around the psyche of Arturo Cova – however strange and unusual some critics may find this mind to be. I think that Ciro Alegría, for example, does wrong to condemn the novel for its lack of psychological development.

I should like to counter-propose that, as in the novel of the land, the selva (as Cova portrays it) is coloured by his troubled and changing outlook from the first page of the novel. His growing involvement in the political problems of his country and his later perceived role as a social redeemer stem from his curiously complex psyche. So too in the chapters that follow, the mythical and archetypal quest (see Chapter 4) is rooted in the natural tendency of Arturo Cova as an individual, and on the higher plane as Everyman, to transcend the purely personal in time and place and reflect the universality of eternal truth. It is also because of his evolving character, with all its defects and virtues, that Cova's odyssey through the jungle, with all its vicissitudes, becomes more than a pursuit of a woman and her abductor transformed into his symbolic enemy, but a search for ideals and values and the realization of dreams and illusions (Chapter 5). The fact that the novel is narrated by the strangely complicated, multisided protagonist, prone to psychological ups and downs, extremes, contradictions, and aberrations, as I shall demonstrate in this chapter, reflects the kind of novel that *La vorágine* is, with its unpre-

dictable, undefinable, uncategorizable genre (seen by many critics to
be lacking in order), which influences the form, the structure, the
style, and the narrative technique (Chapter 6). Thus I stress the importance of this chapter on the psychological development, since the
various dimensions and components of the novel depend totally on
the psyche of Cova. The odyssey is his, and his description of it
is the novel. He is the narrator, and everything is seen through his
eyes, however wild and demented he may seem to some critics: cf.
Bull's views *(3)*, treated in Chapter 1. I shall deal with this problem
of the narrator, however untrustworthy or unreliable he may be, in
Chapter 6.

In *La vorágine* there are few Vargas Llosian tricks of sleight of
hand or withholding of information. From the first words of the
novel Cova reveals his impulsive, impetuous nature: 'Antes que me
hubiera apasionado por mujer alguna, jugué mi corazón al azar y me
lo ganó la Violencia' (11). Faced with an easy conquest, Alicia, disapproving parents, and uncooperative laws in a hypocritical society,
Cova's decision is simple: '¡Huyamos! ... ¡Y huimos!' (11). This
early flight with Alicia to Casanare, for what seems to many critics
no good, convincing reason, is symptomatic of the kind of man that
we shall see throughout the rest of the novel. Incapacitated by
insomnia on his first night, his self-questioning and self-analysis
(after an action taken, it seems, without much thought) prefigure
many such 'reflexiones agobiadoras' on his destiny, on Alicia's role
and his selfish attitude to her, his dreams of glory, and his desire for
success and fame (see Chapter 5).

Arturo Cova, of course, is not José Eustasio Rivera, and one
ought not to read *La vorágine* as Rivera's autobiography. Although
one should beware of too much preoccupation with autobiographical matters in the creation of fiction, it is not possible – nor desirable, some would say – to have the artist refine himself out of existence. What Leon Edel has said about James Joyce applies equally to
Rivera, or any other novelist: 'The disassociation is not complete. He
[the artist] remains after all within, behind, above or beyond the
work – and not too far beyond . . . So a work of fiction, if not autobiography of the artist, is still a particular synthesis created by him
and by no one else.'[6] Whilst being mindful of the dangers of trying
to read into Cova's actions and attributing to them motives to be

[6]*The Psychological Novel 1900-50* (Philadelphia: Lippincott, 1955), p. 179.

found in the life of Rivera, I shall, following my argument detailed above, have occasion to refer to the trajectory of Rivera's own turbulent life to explain, interpret or comment on some parts of this very complex, multi-layered novel.

In his unashamedly psychiatrically-oriented study of the novel (*29*), especially in the section on 'El artista', Mauro Torres interprets the initial flight of Cova and Alicia as a return to the old world of primary emotions. So early in the narrative, then, we are plunged into the insomniac world of Cova, forced to remember and reconstruct already a world of illusions, grief and pain, now compounded by a double responsibility for having almost abducted Alicia and run off to the jungle without a thought for her future. Again at this early stage the reader is confronted with the protagonist's self-questioning about her role in his life, and how they alone against adversity will cope with their fate. As I shall demonstrate in Chapter 6, the fact that he is of the city, cultured, and a poet will obviously have a bearing on the kind of autobiography or memoirs (as the mental ramblings are originally) which this manuscript will finally become. Having made the decision to flee with Alicia, Cova, in some of the best quiet psychological passages of the novel, seeks to analyse and justify not only his actions but her role in the scheme of things (23-24), in his search for the chimera (human as it has to be), the illusions from which, he hopes, will come the triumphs.

In the face of the barbaric conduct of the *enganchador*, Narciso Barrera (whose symbolic name reminds us again of his role as an obstacle between Cova and his ideal woman), appears the first of many bad dreams caused even at this early stage by the combined effect of nature (still relatively benign), jealousy, illness and, of course, an already unstable mind, in which Alicia is portrayed in one scene as fleeing to a sinister place to meet a man (Barrera). The gun in Cova's hand is changed into 'una serpiente helada y rígida' (34). In the same dream Cova sees Alicia naked and fleeing. As he takes the hatchet to pierce the tree for the rubber to trickle out, he hears a voice: '¿Por qué me desangras? ... Yo soy tu Alicia y me he convertido en una parásita' (35). Even the most elementary Freudian analysis of this dream reveals Alicia as the beleagured ideal mother figure of the Romantic hero. Rivera's skill is seen in his portraying of Alicia as the ravished mother/tree figure, which looks back to the exploitation theme of Chapter 2 and forward to the Jungian interpretation of Chapter 4. (For a detailed psychoanalytical view of this event, see *29*, pp. 182-83.) It is no secret that Rivera, who never married nor enjoyed a successful relationship with any of his various girlfriends, had a very ambiguous relationship with his mother (blessed with 'el don de mando'), and his over-affectionate and protective sisters. Rivera, in fact, died at the age of forty without having found the perfect lover or wife.

If Alicia proves finally to be Cova's long-sought-after woman, the protagonist's first confrontation with Barrera (35-36) is also significant, since he turns out to be (apart from the epitome of self-centredness and cruelty) the obstacle between Cova and Alicia, later to be sanctified by maternity. Although Cova knows Barrera's reputation, he confesses that he was impressed by the villain's elegant appearance, smooth talk and adulatory manner as he praises the protagonist for his poetic skills and physical charms. Mauro Torres, in his psychoanalytical approach to the novel, suggests that although Cova's homosexual attraction to Barrera is not explicit (*29*, p. 183), Cova, for fear of being accused thus, immediately and deliberately goes on the offensive. Cova, whose first instinct is to disguise the jealousy which he obviously feels for this powerful man, reacts with an excess of bravura and violence that bespeaks not only his impulsiveness but his desire to emulate the strength and manliness of the llaneros. Cova's symbolic smashing of the bottle of perfume given to Alicia by Barrera sets the scene for the future struggle between Cova and his archetypal enemy for the soul and the body of Alicia. The psychoanalyst might say, of course, that Cova's pursuit of Barrera is an attempt to kill the repressed seducer in his own psyche. But one has the impression, from Cova's own admission, that he seldom suppressed such feelings (42). That he should so soon after this episode encourage la niña Griselda, the wife of his best friend, Fidel Franco (also symbolically named), to fall in love with him 'con éxito escandaloso' (42), underlines this dual aspect of his character which has been explicit from the first page of the novel.

The good side of his character emerges alternately with the other, and feeling guilty about deceiving his best friend ('. . . la lealtad me dominó la sangre, y con desdén hidalgo puse en fuga la tentación', 42), Cova starts to appreciate, even to idealize Alicia, especially since she is now the object of another man's attention, and thus becomes even more desirable. The aforementioned passion and idealization, provoked by jealousy against Barrera, is transcended by her new role and admirable condition − 'la certeza de la futura maternidad' (43). She becomes even more desirable when she treats Cova not only with indifference but even with scarcely disguised disdain. The implied maternity theme becomes explicit in Cova's questioning of Alicia as to her coldness. Provoked into an answer as to how he (Cova) compares with Barrera as a man and lover, Alicia replies, quoting the opinion of la niña Griselda, that Cova is inferior to Barrera. With his pride severely damaged, Cova transforms Barrera into a definitive symbol of his enmity, the complex object of his relentless pursuit. Or as Mauro Torres puts it, Cova becomes the permanent hunter of the hunter who stole his prey (*29*, p. 184). Barrera's strong-man image is also a reminder of the influence of two other strong men in Cova's life, his father and General Reyes. This may help to explain in part 'su rabia importante delante del hombre fuerte', like Colonel Funes, El Cayeno, and General Váquiro.

This kind of psycho-criticism, interesting, powerful and effective as it may be, is doubly efficacious (and complex) in that the psychological analysis is autobiographical and narrated in the first person. That Cova should reflect the *idealidad/realidad* conflict of Rivera's own life becomes the stuff of the search for values (to be treated in Chapter 5). Faced with the reality of his situation in the plains, the poet-dreamer Cova conjures up pictures of literary and financial success, only to admit quickly that fortune and love are mere illusions. The reality is pain and death (45).

Recognizing that his nervous sensibility has passed through several grave crises in which reason tries to divorce itself from the brain, Cova describes lucidly and shrewdly the symptoms of his own 'mal de pensar':

> Frecuentemente las impresiones logran su máximum de potencia en mi excitabilidad, pero una impresión suele degenerar en la contraria a los pocos minutos de recibida. Así, con la música, recorro la gama del entusiasmo para descender luego a las más refinadas melancolías; de la cólera paso a la transigente mansedumbre, de la prudencia a los arrebatos de la insensatez.

En el fondo de mi ánimo acontece lo que en las bahías: las
mareas suben y bajan con intermitencia. (49)

With a penetrating subjectivity, Cova reaches the heights (depths?) of
a character from Dostoievsky or Kafka. Torres suggests that he has
but two alternatives: seek catharsis through the destruction of his
objective (Barrera); or sink into a deeper madness. Even Cova's
drunkenness stems from boredom or curiosity — just so that he can
experience a new sensation.

The departure of Don Rafo, the conscious and civilized voice of
Cova and another representative of the wise old man figure, like
Clemente Silva (cf. Chapter 4), produces in him 'vago pensar, augu-
rio de males próximos, certidumbre de ausencia eterna' (49). This
feeling coincides with his rapid psychological collapse and his awareness that he is passing not only from one psychological stage but
from one physical region to another — from the plain to the symbolic wasteland which is going to have a corresponding maleficent influence on his behaviour: 'Yo entendí que ese desierto tenía algo que
ver con mi corazón' (49). It is not surprising that Cova, worn out,
sad and nervous, allows his jealousy to dominate him to the extent
that he threatens to kill his rival Barrera in Alicia's presence. The
mixture of jealousy, alcohol and anger produces delirious homicidal
and suicidal tendencies: '¡Matarlo! ¡Matarlo! ¡Y después a ti, y a mí
y a todos! ¡No estoy loco! ¡Ni tampoco digan que estoy borracho!
¿Loco? ¡No! ¡Mientes! ¡Loco no! ¡Quítame ese ardor que me
quema el cerebro! ¿Dónde estás? ¡Tiéntame! ¿Dónde estás?' (55).
Then in one of the several hallucinatory scenes of the novel (cf. the
tree-snake dream) he describes, whilst laughing like a madman, his
delirious state: 'Convencido de que era un águila agitaba los brazos y
me sentía flotar en el viento, por encima de las palmeras y de las
llanuras. Quería descender para levantar en las garras a Alicia, y lle-
varla sobre una nube, lejos de Barrera y de la maldad. Y subía tan al-
to, que contra el cielo aleteaba, el sol me ardía el cabello y yo aspir-
aba al ígneo resplandor' (55). The comparison with Franz Kafka's
metamorphosis and Castel's vision of himself as a giant bird in Ernesto Sábato's *El túnel* is not tenuous. The eagle motif (a favourite of
Rivera's poems in *Tierra de promisión*) constitutes one of the most
important symbols of Rivera's search-for-ideals dimension (Chapter

5), not to mention the mythological links with Icarus who aspired to fly, but paid the penalty of approaching too closely to the sun. As the Alicia/snake/parasite nightmare (34-35) signalled the initial crisis, the second dream (eagle/convulsion) aggravates the crisis and acts as a prophetic symbol of Alicia's flight with Barrera (already suggested and foreseen in the first dream).

Now clearly unbalanced after the delirium crisis, Cova, in the wake of the insomniac, homicidal and suicidal tendencies, the hallucinations, and alcoholic excesses, falls victim to somnambulism and repeated self-doubts, self-pity, self-flagellation and self-questioning: 'Un sentimiento de rencor me hacía odioso el recuerdo de Alicia, la responsable de cuanto pasaba . . . Así, con la sinrazón de este razonamiento, envenenaba mi ánima y enconaba mi corazón. ¿Verdaderamente me habría sido infiel? ¿Hasta qué punto le habría mareado el espíritu la seducción de Barrera? ¿Habría existido esa seducción? ¿A qué hora pudo llegarle la influencia del otro?' (61-62).

Hallucinating because of his obsession, and physically exhausted by the fever, feeling alternately guilty (72) and maudlin (73), Cova tries to suppress his feelings of anger. But a letter of apology from Barrera does nothing to soothe his nerves or assuage his thirst for revenge, since basically Barrera represents all that is evil, not only in terms of social exploitation, but in personal terms, as the tempter, the seducer, the abductor of his ideal woman. In psychological and mythical terms he also symbolizes the object to be destroyed, the monster to be killed before the hero attains the holy grail: 'Mas la certidumbre de la venganza, la posibilidad de causarle a mi enemigo algún mal, ponía viveza en mis ojos, ingenio en mis palabras, ardentía en mi decisión' (67-68).

In a moment of weakness Cova is tempted once again by the illusion of attaining perfect love with Alicia and staying to grow old with her in the fascinating region of the plains, free from 'las vanas aspiraciones, del engaño de los triunfos efímeros' (74), not to mention the corrupt cities, surrounded by his children, and slowly dying naturally of old age in the face of glorious sunrises, and in the midst of a beautiful, sympathetic nature. The reality, of course, is the green hell of the jungle which he is about to enter.

After this moment of illusory love and happiness, the poet is faced with the reality that Alicia has departed with Barrera — will-

ingly, as far as Cova knows. Soon the initial tears and self-pity give
way to the psychological outburst or hurricane which constitutes
more or less the rest of the novel: ' . . . estalló mi despecho como un
volcán, y saltando al potro, partí enloquecido para darles alcance y
muerte' (93). Prompted by this emotional outburst, Fidel Franco
sets fire to his own house and ranch, a symbol of the destruction of
Cova's illusions about domestic bliss, riches and family life. Tempted
to throw himself into the flames, then alarmed by his own 'demen-
cia', Cova decides instead that they should pursue the fugitives and
avenge the offence to their honour. The chapter ends in a welter of
emotions, and a purging of weaknesses, with a powerful, infernal
holocaust scene rarely equalled in Latin-American (or any other)
literature:

> El tranquido de los arbustos, el ululante coro de las sierpes y
> de las fieras, el tropel de los ganados pavóricos, el amargo olor
> a carnes quemadas, agasajáronme la soberbia; y sentí deleite
> por todo lo que moría a la zaga de mi ilusión, por ese océano
> purpúreo que me arrojaba entre la selva aislándome del mundo
> que conocí, por el incendio que extendía su ceniza sobre mis
> pasos.
>
>   ¿Qué restaba de mis esfuerzos, de mi ideal y de mi ambi-
> ción? ¿Qué había logrado mi perseverancia contra la suerte?
> ¡Dios me desamparaba y el amor huía! . . .
>
>   ¡En medio de las llamas empecé a reír como Satanás! (94)

With illusions, ideals, ambition, love all gone, and God helpless
or unwilling to assist the hero, Part 1 concludes with a climax
which is a curious mixture of Romantic challenge and despair,
with hints of a Miltonic luciferism. Until this key stage of the
novel, the evolution of Arturo Cova's psyche has taken its full
course, reaching its satanic peak, as a result of basic character defects, his attitude to love and women, and the growing influence
of a hostile and debilitating environment.

Since everything blows up and reaches its demonic climax at
the end of Part 1, it is not surprising that Part 2 of the novel represents a kind of psychological pause or lull before passing on to
the crashing finale and the reconciliation of Cova with Alicia and

his son at the end of Part 3. If Part 1 ends with the satanic outburst, as Cova enters into the jungle, Part 2 begins with his well known apostrophe to the selva (95-96). As Cova makes his way along the 'camino oscuro que se moviera hacia el vórtice de la nada' (98), the somnambulistic misanthropy is particularized and transformed into a vituperative attack on Alicia's character and appearance: 'Ella había sido un mero incidente en mi vida loca y tuvo el fin que debía tener. ¡Barrera merecía mi gratitud!' (101). Although obviously trying to convince himself of her unworthiness, Cova cannot quite rid himself of his feelings for her. Thus one sees two basic psychological attitudes dominating his conduct — sadness and hatred. But it is a confused, ambivalent feeling in which his vengeful anger and his disillusionment with love is mixed with a nostalgic, even illusory, look at his past sentimental life (102). Under the growing influence of his thirst for revenge against Barrera and Alicia, plus the hostility of the land, the homicidal and suicidal tendencies of Part 1 are renewed: 'El fantasma impávido del suicidio, que sigue esbozándose en mi voluntad, me tendió sus brazos esa noche . . . Lenta y oscuramente insistía en adueñarse de mi conciencia un demonio trágico. Pocas semanas antes, yo no era así . . . ' (112).

Interesting as these revelations of Cova's psychological evolution may be, they become even more significant when the reader bears in mind that these descriptions are the confessions of the unbalanced protagonist himself. With the confirmatory report from Helí Mesa that Alicia has been abducted by Barrera, Cova's thoughts turn again to his own possible paternity, the sexual role of Alicia in Barrera's entourage, and his desire for revenge. Recognizing Alicia as the mother-figure clarifies his opposition to Barrera who becomes a symbol of all his rivals and enemies. It is this complicated mixture of his ambivalent thoughts about Alicia, linked psychologically and sexually with his vision of Barrera, not to mention the fever-inspiring 'selvas, siempre interminables y agresivas' (119), which causes Cova to fall 'en un colapso sibilador y mi cabeza desangrándose bajo mis uñas' (117).

Faced with the realization of his growing mental imbalance, the awareness of the hallucination in his brain, Cova comes to the conclusion that he must do something positive to remedy the situation: 'Nunca he conocido pavura igual a la del día que sorprendí a la alu-

cinación en mi cerebro' (121). When he finally admits that his problem is much more than fatigue or fever, as his friends suggest, Cova
makes the illuminating discovery: '... yo comprendía que se tra-
taba de algo más grave y hacía esfuerzos poderosos de sugestión para
convencerme de mi normalidad' (122). These two pages of tortured
self-questioning and self-awareness are amongst the best in the whole
psychological evolution of the protagonist, who wrestles with a psychic phenomenon which he does not fully understand, but whose
very incomprehensibility he articulates with compelling lucidity. His
Romantic explanation, '¡Era lo fatal, lo irremediable!' (122), is the
stuff of the pathological hero, as Luis Eyzaguirre labels and defines
Cova (*9*, p. 83). In the light of his theory, which is based on George
Ross Ridge's *The Hero in French Romantic Literature* (Athens:
University of Georgia Press, 1959), Eyzaguirre considers Cova psychologically convincing in defeat, but more a victim of the demon of
hypersensitivity than of the jungle. This critic, like Bull (*3*), errs in
trying to isolate the mind of the character from the geographical situation which in no uncertain manner is a formative influence. Of
course, Cova has a basic mental condition, as I have suggested
throughout this chapter, but to deny that this condition is exacer-
bated by the hostility of the selva is to underestimate one of the fundamental components of Rivera's complex novel. As Callan points
out (*5*, p. 16), the jungle can be a test which brings out the best or
the worst in a character. Some critics (Ciro Alegría, for example)
find it difficult to accept the changes in the mood of Cova as psychologically consistent. But, as Eyzaguirre explains, these contradic-
tory states are merely the reflection of the conflict between his reason and his sensibility. And the pathological state, because it is just
that, cannot be explained by means of schemes which are consistent
with normality. It is a pity that Eyzaguirre undercuts his own case
by underestimating the importance of the selva as a contributory
factor in the evolution of Cova's psyche.

When his morbid, poetic mind appreciates and praises the beauty
of the death of some shipwrecked comrades, Cova remains perplexed
at the attitude of Fidel Franco who cannot comprehend his apparently inhuman reaction: '¡Todo por ser yo un desequilibrado tan impulsivo como teatral!' (127). The realization that not only is he unbalanced, but that his friends consider him so, is like a hammer-blow

to Cova. Confused and uncertain, he thinks again of Alicia and decides that the odyssey, the search for the ideal woman (which is increasingly materializing in his mind) has to be continued — with all its striving, struggling and deadly implications: 'Claramente, desde aquel día tuve el presentimiento fatal. Todas las desgracias que han sucedido se me anunciaron en ese momento' (131). With this typically Romantic confession, the pathological hero sets out on his destructive and redemptive mission.

If Part 2, as represented by the Silva story, constitutes most of the social-document theme, it does prepare the way for the continuation of Cova's trajectory by plunging him further into the jungle in his quest for Alicia and Barrera, the latter now being seen not only as a personal enemy but as an obstacle to true social justice. The further Cova enters the jungle, the more his psychological state becomes unbalanced, and he continues to doubt his sanity. The hypersensitivity of the pathological hero may be to blame for much of Cova's attitude toward nature, but there is no avoiding the reality of the jungle in all its wildness and cruelty (175). It is a credit to Rivera's skill that he succeeds in portraying the ambivalent combination of the product of Cova's mind with the objective reality of a hostile nature. As Cova proceeds through this inimical forest, the earlier theme of general revenge ('¡Pero yo era la muerte y estaba en marcha!', 118) becomes individualized in his obsession with killing Barrera (in the presence not only of Alicia, but of the rubber-workers, thus fusing the two levels, personal and social): '¡Matar a un hombre!' (178). This becomes his destiny. Possessed by the desert, he is now falling into the vortex of the selva, which claims yet another victim.

Cova's relationship with Zoraida Ayram (reverse form of Maria), la Madona (ironically named), lends itself to various interpretations, given Rivera's equally complex relationship with his mother and sisters. As her name suggests, Ayram, la Madona, is the opposite of the pure, ideal woman, the antithesis of the virgin/mother figure, who has bewitched and destroyed many men, including Don Clemente's son. Although Cova recognizes that la Madona is more interested in material riches and commercial success than in his person, he cannot help being tempted and seduced by her 'prometedora sensualidad' (199). Although promiscuous and greedy, Zoraida, through the

mysterious music of her accordion, not only evokes nostalgia and
melancholy in Cova, but also touches his poetic soul. In this way, he
feels what her music means to the lost and homesick caucheros —
'una promesa de redención' (201). Separated from love, happiness,
his own mother, and his now apparently lost wife Alicia, Cova succumbs to the charms and wiles of la Madona: 'Intenté quererla, como
a todas, por sugestión. ¡La bendije, la idealicé!' (202). But, of
course she is the very antithesis of the ideal woman — vulgar, common, acquisitive, vicious, selfish, lascivious, symbolic of a phallic, sexual stage through which the hero must pass in cathartic fashion
before recognizing the true worth of the ideal woman (225). Only
then, in a moment of nostalgia, does he make the obvious comparison between Alicia and the Turk, recognizing the virtues of the
former, whose previously unappreciated qualities he now begins to
value. When la niña Griselda convinces Cova that Alicia truly is an
honest woman who has not voluntarily abandoned him for Barrera,
nor has she been sold into bondage (on account of her pregnancy),
Cova is now reconciled in his own mind with his ideal woman, and
also with his future son. Once this decision is made, he is free to vent
his rage and hostility on one person, Barrera, the individual and
collective enemy. The rest of the novel prepares the way for what
has been, since mythological times up to the present, the final confrontation between the forces of good and evil, and the removal of
the obstacle by the hero in order to attain his goal.

Before the novel reaches this climax, however, Cova meets with
the last of the complementary narrator-type-foils, Ramiro Estévanez,
a brother/friend/alter ego, whose life had been very closely tied to
his in the past. Ramiro too, because of an affair of the heart, has also
fled the city for the selva; and he too has his illusions about life, love
and the ideal woman. Here in the jungle, where his reversed name,
Esteban Ramírez, symbolizes the complete change in his life and
character, he represents the mirror image of Arturo Cova: 'Siempre
nos veíamos, nunca nos tuteábamos. Él era magnánimo; impulsivo
yo. Él, optimista; yo, desolado. Él, virtuoso y platónico; yo, mun-
dano y sensual. No obstante, nos acercó la desemejanza, y, sin des-
viar las innatas inclinaciones, nos completábamos en el espíritu, po-
niendo yo la imaginación, él la filosofía' (206). A good, noble, kind
soul, because of an unhappy love affair he has fled to the jungle

where he remains sad, reserved, hungry, not to mention symbolically blinded for his crime of having witnessed the San Fernando atrocities committed by Cova's other nemesis, Colonel Funes. (The double implication of the blinded, bandaged eyes — love, justice — is obvious.) It is no wonder that this alter ego of Cova is bitter and sardonic about life in general, and love in particular, since his ideal woman is now married to another, deemed more socially acceptable. Recognizing that Ramírez's situation is exactly the same as his, Cova tries to persuade his friend to join his mission of revenge. The cause is clear, the effect simple, dating back to the violence of the opening page of the novel: '¡Me robé una mujer y me la robaron! ¡Vengo a matar al que la tenga!' (209) — re-echoing the later professed raison d'être of his odyssey — 'Matar a un hombre' (178). It is interesting that Ramírez too notices and underscores the satanic qualities of his proud friend, who is now more than ever determined to have his revenge: 'Mal te cuadre el penacho rojo de Lucifer' (209).

Esteban Ramírez's narrative of the San Fernando massacre serves to shore up the patriotic idealism and social mission of Cova, as well as intensifying the personal thirst for revenge. Barrera, of course, has a special role to play since he transcends the mere system to become a personal enemy and an obstacle to the realization of Cova's dreams. With Alicia beatified by maternity and the regenerative role of the paternity theme confirmed, Cova can now channel all his energy into the final destruction of his antagonist. As Mauro Torres shrewdly points out (*29*, p. 193), Cova could have killed Barrera much earlier in the novel during their first jealous quarrel at la Maporita. But he did not, since the way of the psyche is complicated and devious. The killing of Barrera is tied up with the complex struggle of attaining his idealized and inaccessible woman — a process which takes place only after many complicated adventures (and workings of the human mind), and only at the end of the novel. Cova is now further along his psychological line of development, whereas in human, physical terms, as well as in terms of prestige, Barrera is less strong and more vulnerable at the end of the novel.

With the elimination of Barrera, who signifies throughout the novel the internal and external barrier between Cova and his ideal woman, the odyssey will be almost over, on various levels (personal, socio-political, psychological). But the curve is not complete until the hero performs the final action, motivated by a mixture of jealousy?, revenge?, desire to escape? The questioning is Cova's, as he bares his soul in an outpouring of tormented self-interrogation and confession. All that he knows for certain is that the deed has to be done: 'Definitivamente, desde ese momento me abandonó la paz del espíritu. ¡Matar a un hombre! ¡He aquí mi programa, mi obligación!' (228). His psyche appears to be even more confused at the end than at the beginning, given the relentless influence of an inimical nature, illness and emotional stress. Nervous, hallucinatory, more dead than alive, suffering grievously from beriberi, dismayed at the timidity and the unwillingness of his alter ego to abandon his life of failure and submission, Cova weeps not just for himself but for that part of his persona which he recognizes in his friend, who prefers to remain in the oblivion of the jungle in order to suppress the deceptions of life, especially his unrequited love for the unattainable woman. Unable to persuade Ramírez to join him in his escape with Alicia to a new life, Cova draws comfort, denied to his alter ego, from the consolation of a hard-earned union, attained by the destruction of the constant obstacle and sanctified by the saving grace of motherhood (243).

The final struggle between the hero and his nemesis is appropriately gigantic, even cosmic in its proportions — 'tremenda, muda, titánica' (247) — and suitably gruesome, as we have seen. If Cova's aim in life is to kill a man, specifically Barrera, now at the end he can state triumphantly and proudly: 'Ya libré a mi patria del hijo infame. Ya no existe el enganchador. ¡Lo maté! ¡Lo maté!' (247). But even before he rids himself and his country of this selfish monster, he reiterates the pathological Romantic hero's tragic awareness of his presence at the edge of the abyss, the chasm of life: 'Tengo el presentimiento de que mi senda toca a su fin, y, cual sordo zumbido de ramajes en la tormenta, percibo la amenaza de la vorágine' (246).

In spite of the several references to the satanic character of the protagonist, by the end of the novel the psychological line has taken a dramatic curve. The satanic figure of the early part of the novel has become almost messianic, at least in the eyes of the exploited workers whom he defends in their hopeless struggle against the forces of evil. After the death of Barrera in what Cova himself calls a titanic struggle, thus raising the level of the contest above the merely personal and national to an almost cosmic level (good versus evil), Cova rejects the 'redentor' title and the social-saviour label which his unfortunate compatriots have seen fit to bestow on him — a far cry from the impulsive, selfish, theatrical, homicidal, satanic image which he revealed in earlier pages of the novel. He admits that in other circumstances he would have sacrificed himself for his fellow-countrymen, but at the end, after seven months of anger, sadness, hatred and revenge, he makes the conscious decision and the personal choice of responsible fatherhood to protect the health of his family — so that his son's life may not be endangered by contact with the very masses for whom he has long struggled.

With the catharsis complete, and the alternative total madness apparently avoided, the psychological curve, the analytical process, the spiritual odyssey, and the narrative itself, all come to a close. The evolution of the mind of Arturo Cova is fascinating and harrowing to behold. It becomes even more interesting from the perspective of the autobiographical format that Rivera has used for the novel. The psyche of Arturo Cova is strange and complex. To have it depicted in the first person by the unbalanced, perhaps unreliable narrator contributes not only to the ambiguity of the self-confession, self-justification, self-condemnation of the volatile, ambivalent protagonist, but to the powerful effect that *La vorágine* has as a universal work of art. This is a novel which transcends the plains, the desert, and the jungle of Colombia, the unique physical background against which Rivera paints the convincing struggle of human passions. But by also skilfully using the geography of his native land to influence the impressionable mind of the protagonist, Rivera increases the efficacy and the success of *La vorágine* as a psychological novel.

4 *The Quest Motif*

If, as I have suggested, *La vorágine* transcends local and national frontiers to become a universal work of art, it is because of Rivera's convincing depiction not only of Cova's mind, but of all the conflicting human passions. It is this overall rendering of the qualities common to all mankind which raises the novel to the heights of great literature. Also, I have already alluded to the character of Cova as a manifestation of the Romantic hero, whilst the selva serves as a symbol of the hostile universe against which man struggles. What I am proposing here is that *La vorágine*, in the light of our new knowledge in the field of psychology and psychiatry, and especially in our new awareness of the importance of myths, types, archetypes and symbols, can be examined afresh, reinterpreted and reappraised. The fact that this novel has been subject to various individual studies in the last twenty years or so from the differing points of view of Freudian, Jungian and overtly Christian interpretations, not to mention the pagan Greek and Roman mythological perspectives, confirms my view that it is a rich, multi-layered work of art, rooted in myth, which speaks to all times, not least our own.

Mythological Beginnings: Virgil

If one can accept the rough general definition of a myth as an eternal truth, or as Mark Schorer describes it, as a 'large controlling image that gives philosophic meaning to the facts of ordinary life',[7] one has no difficulty in interpreting *La vorágine* as a twentieth-century version of the quest myth. Northrop Frye has defined the crucial stages of the quest myth thus: i) perilous journey (*agon*); ii) crucial struggle (*pathos*); iii) exaltation of the hero (*anagnorisis*).[8] The application of this theory of myth to Cova's odyssey through the selva,

[7] *The Study of Literature: A Handbook of Critical Essays and Terms* (Boston: Little, Brown, 1960), p. 315.
[8] *Anatomy of Criticism* (Princeton: University Press, 1957), p. 187.

his battle to the death with Barrera, and his reunion with Alicia, the birth of his son, and his recognition as a hero, is self-evident. By the end of the novel, as I have already suggested, after the titanic struggle with Barrera, the monstrous, sinister, dragon figure of mythology, Cova has attained mythical proportions not only as a social redeemer but as a messianic hero figure. It is no coincidence that his struggle with the animal world of the jungle, portrayed in terms of monsters or wild beasts of prey (jackals, vultures, wolves, tigers) reaches biblical heights. As Frye points out (p. 149), in demonic societies, represented by Egypt and Babylon, their rulers, like Pharaoh and Nebuchadnezzar, are represented as beasts, often the dragon figure (cf. Perseus, St George) or the sea-monster of the Bible, Leviathan (cf. Jonah and the whale). The fact that already in a brief introductory paragraph I have managed to encompass contemporary social problems, biblical parallels, and mythological origins, all within the framework of a summary discussion of *La vorágine*, would seem to confirm the very point which I am anxious to make. *La vorágine* is a novel written on various levels which lends itself to several interpretations, based on the assumption that it contains, through a skilful presentation and fusion of mythological figures and archetypal patterns,[9] the long-sought-after eternal truth, susceptible to universal application.

In the previous chapters we witnessed the adventures of Arturo Cova set against the American background, with something of his evolution as an individual and Romantic figure. In this chapter I should like to trace the transfiguration of Cova into a mythic figure, along the lines suggested above. The American protagonist's flight into his own jungle terrritory is transformed (through the magic of art and the eternal truth of myth) into what Leónidas Morales calls 'un viaje al país de los muertos' (*18*), or the descent into the underworld of the selva, 'la catedral de la pesadumbre, donde dioses desconocidos hablan a media voz' (95).

The descent into Hell motif is, as Mircea Eliade has described it,[10] as old as history itself, and has been developed in many myths

---

[9]Frye's definition of an archetype is eminently suitable for our purposes here: 'a symbol, usually an image, which recurs often enough in literature to be recognizable as an element of one's literary experience as a whole' (p. 365).
[10]For example, *Myths, Dreams and Mysteries* (New York: Harper, 1960).

and primitive rites. In our western literary tradition it has been best portrayed by Homer, Virgil and Dante, as an elaboration of the Greek myth of the River Styx. It is to his credit that Morales was suggesting as early as 1965 (at a time when the admirers and exponents of the new novel were condemning works like *La vorágine* to the nether regions of irrelevance and oblivion) the possibility of some link between *La vorágine* and certain myths, especially the Stygian, which had been presented by Homer in the *Odyssey*, Virgil in the *Aeneid*, and when we move from the world of mythology to literature, in the *Divine Comedy* of Dante. (The story of Christ's descent into Hell suggests another dimension, which is basic to the Dante version.) In other words, through the aforementioned fundamental intertextuality (see my Introduction, p. 11), one can safely say that there would be no *Divine Comedy* without the *Aeneid*, and no *Aeneid* without the *Odyssey*. And, of course, it goes without saying that if there are formal, structural, symbolic and archetypal links between *La vorágine* and Virgil and Dante, they are explained by the mythological substratum which presupposes fundamental human experiences shared by all men in all societies. The original Greek myth describes metaphorically one of the basic experiences, which has since been identified in literature as the quest myth, or journey. The fact that Rivera's protagonist uses expressions like 'odisea' (216) to describe his adventures, 'titánica' (247) to describe his crucial final struggle, or 'dantesca' (248) to describe the death scene of his antagonist, is a mere illustration of the poetic manifestations of the modern treatment of the mythical experiences.

Taking as his guide the Virgilian outline of the five basic elements of composition, Morales (*18*, pp. 159-62) identifies all five elements present in *La vorágine*: (i) The dark waters of the River Styx – 'Aquel río, sin ondulaciones, sin espumas, era mudo, tétricamente mudo como el presagio y daba la impresión de un camino oscuro que se moviera hacia el vórtice de la nada' (98) (cf. *Aeneid*, Canto VI). (ii) The boat of Charon which transports the souls of the dead – 'La curiara, como un ataúd flotante, siguió agua abajo . . . esta curiara parece un féretro' (98); 'Llegamos a las márgenes del río Vichada derrotados por los zancudos. Durante la travesía los azuzó la muerte tras de nosotros y nos persiguieron día y noche, flotando en halo fatídico y quejumbroso, trémulos como una cuerda a medio vibrar ' (111). (iii) The opposite shore (cf. *Aeneid*, Canto VI, and Dante's *Inferno*, Canto III, 14-18); Cova is fearful on approaching the opposite bank of the river: 'Por mi parte, sólo os demando que me ayudéis a ganar la opuesta margen' (130). (iv) The guide – when they reach the other shore they meet Clemente Silva, who is to be their guide in the jungle. (v) Hell – the green hell of the jungle is conceived of as a prison surrounded by rivers which seem like deep ditches or moats: 'ignoráis la tortura de vagar sueltos en una cárcel como la selva, cuyas bóvedas verdes tienen por muros ríos inmensos' (170). Even the guide gets lost in the internal prison labyrinth which resembles the sinister forest in Milton's *Comus*, or, more properly in this comparison, the opening lines of the *Inferno*. The reference to the labyrinth, the image of lost direction, often with a monster like the Minotaur at its centre, transcends another set of myths. For Northrop Frye, whose interest in mythology is deeply rooted in the Bible, the labyrinthine wanderings of the Old Testament Jews in the desert is repeated in the New Testament by Jesus in the company of the Devil or wild beasts, and fits the same pattern.

If at times I use the word 'Dantesque' to describe the kinds of situations which prevail in *La vorágine*, I do so in the knowledge that there is an element of presupposition in our appreciation of the *Inferno*, which depends to a great extent on our recognition that it descends from the *Aeneid* and hence from the *Odyssey*. This way of looking at the modern novel in the light of past literature, mythology and the Bible, is suggestively fruitful, and enriches our psychological reading of the novel, as I indicated in Chapter 3.

It is no coincidence that Latin-American literature of the post-1950 era has been greatly enriched by the new novelists' response to Carlos Fuentes' clarion call to create a new literature rooted in poetry and myth. In *La vorágine* Rivera has united the geographical and temporal past, thus anticipating Asturias, Carpentier, Rulfo, García Márquez and others, by a subtle fusion of the folkloric and the mythological, the regional and the universal. In what purports to be a novel set in the Colombian jungle and dealing with social abuses prevalent in the early twentieth century, Rivera has revealed in the character of Cova his capacity for handling the concerns of all mankind from time immemorial. The fact that he has used the eternal truth of myth as developed from earliest societies and civilizations, religions and literatures, manifested in the works of the greatest exponents of past cultures, like Homer, Virgil, Dante, is a sign of the universal character of *La vorágine*.

Myth to Theology: Dante

In the previous section I pointed out links with the great works of classical mythology, the *Odyssey* and the *Aeneid*, in the framework of which one can see *La vorágine* as an extension of the eternal truths of these myths, whose structures, themes and figures are important to the Colombian work's status as more than a telluric novel of political denunciation. In his trek through the jungle Arturo Cova has already been compared to Virgil's Aeneas, and by extension to his predecessor, Homer's Odysseus. Although this archetypal comparison with the great mythical heroes is, of course, the key to a more than superficial reading of the novel, other classical analogies and allusions abound. From the first paragraph of the novel Cova, through the sin of pride, seeks in Promethean fashion to steal the divine fire of ideal love (cf. the treatment of Lucifer and Adam in biblical and literary terms in the Book of Genesis and Milton's *Paradise Lost*): 'ambicionaba el don divino del amor ideal, que me encendiera espiritualmente, para que mi alma destellara en mi cuerpo como la llama sobre el leño que la alimenta' (11). When Alicia later becomes the embodiment of this idealized love, Cova in his delirium portrays himself as an eagle, anxious to swoop down and snatch up Alicia in his claws and carry her away on a cloud far from Barrera and harm. Icarus-like in his eagerness, he flies too close to the sun and pays the penalty for his pride, as we saw in Chapter 3. The classical correspondence is extended beyond Cova to his travelling companions in distress, e.g. his faithful companion Fidel Franco is a reflection of Aeneas' loyal friend, Achates. Seymour Menton, who has commented knowledgeably on this aspect of the novel, points out the similarity between Cova's and Fidel's search for Alicia and the efforts of the Greek heroes to liberate Helen who had allowed herself to be carried off by Paris (*17*, p. 427). In a novel where names are all-important as symbols of individuals and types, as I have already pointed out in the cases of Barrera Narciso, Fidel Franco, Clemente Silva, Zoraida Ayram, and others, Arturo Cova himself symbolizes on one hand all that is good and noble in the legend of King Arthur, while Cova, as we have seen, and as we shall see even more profoundly in the next (Jungian) interpretation, symbolizes the cave, or the dark demonic side of man. Menton, whose perceptive remarks on this dimension of the novel I acknowledge throughout this section, has made a detailed but at times tentative study of the names and their significance.

By means of an imaginative, but at times inconsistent, study of *La vorágine* in terms of Dante's work, Menton raises the Colombian novel to the heights of a 'complex pessimistic Christian vision of man's fall from Paradise and his punishment and ultimate death in the concentric circles of Hell' (*17*, p. 418). As Morales had detailed the similarities between the Colombian selva and the black vortex of Virgil's *Aeneid*, Menton identifies it with the 'dark wood' of Dante's *Inferno*. In his openly Christian interpretation of the novel (despite its pessimistic ending), Menton represents Cova as the fallen angel, who, like Lucifer, succumbs to pride, so that by the end of the first part of the novel he manifests his satanic character, as I have already pointed out, in a demonic outburst. However, one also remembers that by the end of the novel he is perceived by his fellow-sufferers to be a kind of redeemer, albeit more social than moral. Eschewing the saviour role, when faced with the birth of his son (not necessarily an optimistic, redemptive feature for Menton, despite the Christian analogy), Cova disappears into the jungle never to be seen again. In *La vorágine*, as in the *Divine Comedy* and in Christian theology (e.g. the Trinity), a tripartite structure is very significant. The geographical structure of the novel (the sierra, the plains, the selva) corresponds to Dante's Paradise, Purgatory and Inferno. As a careful reading shows, the pattern is not perfect, since the regions, like the parts of the novel, overlap to produce the confusion and the lack of order which characterize both the jungle and Rivera's metaphysical vision.

Following the pattern of the *Divine Comedy*, Menton sees the sierra as the equivalent of Paradise, from which the fallen angel was cast out because he aspired to ideal love. This explanation is not quite justified, as Rodney Williamson has also noted (*33*, p. 18), since Cova did not run off to the plain with Alicia for reasons of ideal love. The idealization process takes place only later (see Chapter 3). The theme of the cast-out angel, ironically, fits much better the situation of Cova's alter ego, Esteban Ramírez, as I have demonstrated in Chapter 3. Cova's decision is more an act of bravado and revenge against the conventional families of the two runaways, and society in general. Also, throughout the novel Bogotá is not presented as the Edenic source of light, love and goodness. Cova, like Rivera, had few illusions about the city which for him had many bad memories of hypocrisy, corruption and vice, and was also associated in his mind with his failures, both in love and in art. However, because of its height, the sierra may be regarded as the conventional seat of Paradise, and because of its position in time and place as the source of Arturo's youthful innocence and illusions. It is also the haven to which the traveller-hero returns in memory and nostalgic dreams, happy and successful (financially and artistically), to the bosom of his family and the arms of his loving and forgiving mother. Although this structure is not as successfully drawn as Menton would like to believe, the pattern is useful for a comparison of the two key works.

If the sierra equals Paradise, where all is, theoretically, love and happiness, the plains represent Purgatory, with its ambivalent properties, like Nature itself. In fact, in terms of geographical structure, the hero has already entered the plains of Purgatory in Part 1. In the Christian Dantean Purgatory, souls remain there to suffer for a time, to make reparation for their sins, before finally moving up to Paradise. The difference between Dante's conventional Purgatory and Rivera's is that the contemporary author's place of suffering is seldom seen as a place of transit or preparation for the ascension to Paradise. In Rivera's Purgatory, the plains of Casanare province provide the setting for the first crossing of the River Styx (cf. the *Aeneid*), thus reversing the direction of the odyssey of the Christian travellers. Although Hell proper does not begin in geographical terms until they enter the jungle province of Vichada, Menton concedes that because of the grotesque characters and the fiendish murders, the crossing of the plains could be regarded as the first circle of Hell. The jungle, with its brutal cruelty, dehumanizing slavery, and never-ending exploitation, is an authentic, convincing symbol of Hell.

Clemente Silva is the spokesman for all these downtrodden and ill-treated victims who suffer because of the system. In his narrowly theological view of the novel, Menton offers a rebuttal to those who would interpret it in purely Marxist terms as a bitter indictment of the capitalist system which permits, even condones, such exploitation.[11] In Menton's Christian reading, since the caucheros are on the whole no better than their exploiters, they too are punished for their greed and their maltreatment of their neighbours and the forest. As Cova and his group push further into the second circle of Hell, the power of the jungle, like that of the exploiters, becomes even more destructive, with death present at every step and on every shore. Although he is eventually reunited with his ideal woman, after killing his rival, Cova is still the fallen angel, the false, reluctant redeemer, who puts wife and child before the welfare of the leper colony. In an apparently rash, but explicable, action, he finally leads his wife and child further into the jungle where he is swallowed up – an irrevocable and lasting punishment for his pride. Menton's comparison (*17*, p. 423) of this disappearance with Ulysses' ship whirled round three times before being gobbled up by the sea is apt (cf. *Inferno*, Canto XXVI). Both suffer for an act of pride which deceives them into thinking that they can defy Nature and God(s). The ending is pessimistic (in Christian terms) in that the birth of Cova's son is not a source of saving grace, nor is it a redemptive event, as in the archetypal pattern, as Richard Callan has argued (*4*). But Menton undercuts his own thesis somewhat by admitting that Cova is not eternally defiant. He does display a concern for the lepers and other lost souls (the Brazilians) at the end of the novel. This is not the satanic figure of the end of Part 1. At the conclusion of the novel, Arturo Cova is more balanced, more charitable, more socially concerned, more civic-minded, more mature, and generally less selfish – in other words, a better man and a better citizen. That this change should be effected by the attainment of his ideal love and the birth of his son reduces somewhat the pessimistic note struck by Menton in his limiting triangular interpretation of the novel.

When Menton demonstrates and stresses the circular basis and motion of the novel from the stylistic, linguistic and anthropological points of view, the critic is on much firmer ground with his imagery.

[11] See, for example, F.V. Kelin's introduction to the Russian edition (1935), reprinted in *Atenea*, 33 (1936), 314-25.

The whirlpool or vortex of Virgil and Dante, which whirls its victims around before devouring them, is the key image in *La vorágine*. It is interesting and significant that Northrop Frye, in his theory of archetypal meaning, whilst describing the inorganic world, should identify several of the sinister counterparts of the geometrical images (Menton's triangle and circle), for example, the sinister spiral (maelstrom, whirlpool, or Charybdis). The sinister circle is also identified with the serpent, which is, in conventional and biblical terms, a demonic creature (Frye, p. 150). For the Jungian, however, as we shall see in the next section, the serpent with its tail in its mouth, Ouroboros (or Uroboros), is also the archetypal image of happiness, corresponding to preconsciousness, the earliest state of the psyche.

Whether one accepts the total package of Menton's theory or not is irrelevant. It is a tribute to Rivera's skill that Menton is able to provide yet another plausible interpretation of the novel through a Dantean perspective via Homer, Virgil and others, which contributes to the many-dimensional composition of *La vorágine*.

Myth to Archetype: Jung

In Chapter 3 I dealt with the psychological evolution of the protagonist as an unbalanced character. In the light of recent discoveries in archetypal criticism, we can now examine the novel from the perspective of Cova's ability to transcend the purely personal and individual in order not only to encompass mythological and mythical proportions, but also to reach archetypal status. Ironically, Rivera, through Cova, anticipated this capacity of his narrative to reach beyond the socio-political aspects of the novel, important as they were at that time, and as they are on that particular level of creativity and utility: 'Sólo he logrado hacer mitológicos sus padecimientos y novelescas las torturas que los aniquila' (*21*, p. 306). Only by recognizing, examining and identifying the archetypal structure, pattern and meaning of the novel, can we reach yet another level of this prolix work, in the treatment of the 'psychic renewal' (to use Richard Callan's felicitous phrase) of the complex protagonist.

When Emir Rodríguez Monegal discusses the valid tradition of the novel of the land in Latin America, highlighting the aforementioned double link between man and nature, he goes on to speak of 'la elaboración de mitos centrales de un continente que ellos aun veían en su desmesura romántica'.[12] If Doña Bárbara symbolizes the native barbarism, and Don Segundo the strength, independence and stoicism of the gaucho, Arturo Cova is surely much more than an impetuous, misguided do-gooder. In previous chapters we have seen the figure of Cova depicted as the quintessential Romantic hero, whose qualities are translated by Rodríguez Monegal into 'una categorización heroica . . . , una visión arquetípica' (p. 51). If this is the case with *La vorágine*, as I have been arguing, the words of Cova to Clemente Silva have become ironically prophetic: 'Cuente usted con que la novela tendrá más éxito que la historia' (138). In an interesting aside on the genre of *La vorágine*, Rodríguez Monegal, using the criteria set out by Northrop Frye, classifies *La vorágine* (and *Don Segundo Sombra* and *Doña Bárbara*) not as a novel but as a romance, whose typical atmosphere is 'a world in which the ordinary laws of nature are slightly suspended' (Frye, *Anatomy of Criticism*, p. 33). This idea might be used as an argument against William Bull's criticism (*3*, p. 315) of Cova's failure to describe the 'objective reality' of the jungle (*33*, pp. 4-10).

Whatever the generic label, it becomes clear that there is a mythical pattern in *La vorágine*, in which the Romantic traits of the protagonist lend themselves to heroic categorization, and in which the hero becomes myth. There also emerges finally an archetypal structure and vision, whose symbols and stages can be clearly identified by means of the psychological theories of Carl Jung, as Richard Callan has demonstrated admirably in his seminal article (*4*). It should be added that it is in the light of the archetypal interpretation of the novel that Rodríguez Monegal's distinction between novel and romance reveals itself, as Williamson (*33*) points out, in Frye's terms: 'The essential difference between novel and romance lies in the conception of characterization. The romancer does not attempt to create "real people" so much as stylized figures which expand into psychological archetypes. It is in the romance that we find Jung's libido, anima, and shadow reflected in the hero, heroine, and villain respectively' (Frye, p. 304).

---

[12]'La nueva novela latinoamericana' in *Actas del Tercer Congreso Internacional de Hispanistas* (Mexico City: El Colegio de México, for AIH, 1970), pp. 47-63, at p. 51.

In this analysis, in which I follow Callan's argument very closely, *La vorágine* describes the process of Arturo Cova's psychic regeneration, provoked by his relationship with Alicia, and by his great desire to capture his ideal love, to overcome his problem of not being able to relate to women in particular, and people in general. Even so early in the process Cova is astute enough to realize that perhaps the ideal is not to be sought after, since one carries it within one: 'el ideal no se busca; lo lleva uno consigo mismo' (12); or as Jung put it: 'Every man carries within him the eternal image of woman', to which image he gives the name anima, since it animates or inspires him. The search for the ideal love, then, implies a process of regeneration, of renewal, and the liberation of the anima, which is a personification of the suppressed feminine side of man, and which he projects on to the woman he loves. The process consists of facing the collective psyche, the total unconscious in its feminine form, the Great Mother. Obviously Alicia has not successfully carried the projection of Cova's anima, since it tends to dissolve back into the unconscious (cf. Alicia as the tree image, 35) and becomes indistinguishable from the Great Mother – a normal process in the early development of the psyche. Since each level of consciousness is reached only through the self-renewal of symbolic death or sacrifice, Cova has to release his anima through the dragon-fight (cf., in the mythological interpretation, the figures of Theseus and St George). Aware of his need to renew himself, of his search for the Ideal, Cova is prepared to make the sacrifice in order to free the feminine (good, beneficial) image, the anima, represented by Alicia, from the unconscious. Barrera, of course, symbolizes the monster or the dragon which he has to slay, one of the negative representations of the jungle, the Great Mother, which threatens to swallow up the hero.

At the beginning of the novel the anima is weak and easily becomes lost in the unconscious. In Cova's dreams Alicia becomes a tree and is integrated into the selva, into the 'bosque nocturno', i.e. into the Collective Unconscious. When she is separated from him spiritually by her aloofness, and later physically on her departure with Barrera, Cova begins to realize that she does mean something to him, as we have already seen (Chapter 3). Since she is distant and withdrawn, he can now project on to her his ideal, and thus she becomes, as it were, the carrier of this ideal. As in mythology, dreams and rituals are very important in Jungian psychology. Even before she leaves with Barrera, who is already predicated as his enemy, Cova dreams of her going to meet his opponent. When Cova tries to shoot his rival, the gun turns into a snake, an ambiguous symbol of death and life (apart from being a basic demonic figure in the Bible, and a Freudian phallic symbol). Because of its capacity for shedding its skin and thus renewing itself, the snake is also a symbol of rebirth. With Alicia now his anima, Cova follows her through the jungle in his journey not only to take Romantic revenge, but also to undergo a series of tests before the final encounter with Barrera, the last stage of his quest (the dragon-fight of myth and fairy tale), the final proof of his masculinity. In Jungian psychology hero-motifs of this kind are archetypes of transformation and renewal, which exist in the Collective Unconscious and are still applicable to the contemporary situation: 'The dragon-fight . . . occurs whenever in fact a rebirth or a reorientation of consciousness is indicated. For the captive is the "new" element whose liberation makes further development possible' (*4*, p. 472). The labyrinth symbolizes the total unconscious, or Great Mother, which is ambivalent since it has a good and a bad side, represented by the monster and the maiden. The aim is to separate the anima-maiden from the Great Mother-monster. In other words, the selva, 'la vorágine', is equivalent to the dark labyrinthine aspect of the Great Mother; Barrera represents the Minotaur-monster or Terrible Mother; and Alicia is the captive-anima to be liberated.

During his quest-trek when he is being put to the test, Cova resists the sexual temptation of the orgy with the Indian women, thus (surprisingly, given his reputation) demonstrating his self-control and a strengthening of the ego-stability, a temporary victory at least over the unconscious, which is necessary if he is to continue his heroic odyssey. Rivera skilfully makes use again of the Indian mythology, in the legend of Mapiripama, to symbolize the negative side of the anima and instincts out of control. At the climactic end of Part 1 the snake image appears yet again in the firing of Fidel Franco's ranch, when Cova sees the flames twist and turn into the figure of the snake biting its own tail (93). As Callan points out (in opposition to Frye's theory of myth with regard to the serpent, I might add), the circular serpent Uroboros is the archetypal image of original happiness, and corresponds to the earliest psychic stage, the pre-conscious (*4*, p. 472). A prerequisite of the regeneration process or initiation rit-

ual/drama is the death-test, in which the potential hero has to confront the death-situation. Throughout his ordeal, Cova has to experience many flirtations with death in his various fits of delirium,
fevers and hallucinations, not to mention physical fights to the death
with various symbolic and real-life rivals, culminating in the final titanic confrontation with Barrera. In perhaps one of the most harrowing death scenes in the novel, in that the protagonist is describing
his own death, Cova, in a state of catalepsy, feels the cold invading
his body whilst a grim shadow at his side swings its death-bearing
scythe over his head, as his will frantically continues the struggle
with his unresponsive body. Horrified, he awaits the fatal blow from
the grim reaper, and when it does come his skull breaks into a hun-
dred tinkling fragments like the sound of coins in a money-box.
Even more frighteningly, he preserves his senses and hears his friend
Fidel Franco saying coldly: 'Abrid la sepultura, que está muerto. Era
lo mejor que podía sucederle', whilst Cova shouts inaudibly: 'Estoy
vivo, estoy vivo' (123). As Callan suggests, it is important that Cova
should hear this statement at the precise moment of hallucination,
because he has to listen to it in order to resign himself to death so
that he may better aspire to rebirth. In other words, the voice of his
unconscious tells him to die, because psychologically in order to live
this is the experience that he needs most: 'According to Jung, a living tension between the conscious and the unconscious maintains
our psychic balance and reflects the movement of the libido [i.e.
psychic energy].' In mythological terms ' . . . the Great Mother pur-
sues her son with madness until he offers sacrifice to her. When
something of value is given up in sacrifice, energy regresses to the unconscious, provoking a one-sided accumulation. The normal rever-
sion of the psychic process results in a fresh charge of energy for
consciousness' (*4*, p. 473). Until the new release of psychic energy is
received, there is a temporary imbalance — hence Cova's lack of
mental equilibrium, bouts of insanity, hallucinations, deliriums, etc.
In Part 1 of the novel, when Cova obviously needs renewal, he often
acts without restraint. Once his process of renewal begins, his de-
rangement becomes more acute, which is normal in the initial regression, since the psychic energy activates the contents of the unconscious. This explains the host of archetypal images emanating from
Cova's unconscious — the dismemberment image of Barrera's body,

the circular snake, the siren figure, the vital death-scene, which all act as 'transformers of energy', just as the anima does for the hero (*4*, p. 473).

Later persecuted by the trees, Cova again fears for his mental stability. But as he contemplates the mystery of death as a natural phenomenon and the precursor of life, he sees this confirmed all around him in the forest where, in the midst of dead trees and rotting leaves, little seedlings sprout up. His renewed awareness of the cyclical law of nature ('Es la muerte, que pasa dando la vida', 176) is an apt analogy for his own psychic state, which seems to be, at least for the moment, in harmony with nature. As I pointed out in Chapter 1, nature in both its maleficent and its beneficent guise had a great effect on Rivera at various stages in his life, and certainly has an equally profound meaning for his creation, Cova. These ambivalent emotions, generated by the Great Mother, highlight the contrasting aspects, good and evil, positive and negative, of the Good and Terrible Mother figure. This same ambivalence is reflected in Cova's attitude to the fleeing Alicia, for whom his hatred is replaced by feelings of admiration, even love. Although longing for her friendship, he nonetheless deems her good riddance, and deprecates her virtue by conjuring up lewd visions of her engaged in acts of promiscuity, the 'amorío fácil' of the opening page – a sure sign of the immaturity of the anima, and the regression in his psychic stability, reflected in his childish behaviour towards his ideal woman.

If Cova's search for Alicia dominates the first half of the novel (and continues till the end), the hero's quest runs parallel with, and in Part 2 often takes second place to, the narrative of Clemente Silva and his search for his son. In the selva, evoked by Cova variously as 'madre', 'esposa', 'cárcel verde', 'catedral', 'cementerio enorme' (contrasting images which indicate the conflicting nature of the Great Mother, Good and Terrible), Cova meets Don Clemente, another symbol (like Don Rafo, of the early part) of the wise old man, kind, compassionate, sympathetic, the guide of the forest. Rodney Williamson, in his treatment of Callan's Jungian interpretation of the novel, points to other archetypes not developed by Callan (*33*, pp. 20-23). El Pipa, for example, the thieving messenger-rascal of the first part of the novel, is clearly the archetypal trickster, or the *gottliche Schelm* of Jung, corresponding to the god Hermes or Mercury in classical literature. Since the trickster represents the earliest period of life, El Pipa typifies the primitive underdeveloped stage of Cova's psyche, before he learns to see things differently under the tutelage of his mentor-guide, the wise old man, represented by Clemente Silva. In the next stage, when the hero passes to a more active redeemer role, the archetype for this third level is the twin, represented by his kindred spirit, Ramiro Estévanez, his alter ego and psychological complement, as I have demonstrated at length in Chapter 3.

The key figure, then, in Cova's evolution is the spiritual (and physical) guide, Don Clemente, who is in many ways an opposite to Cova, at least in his dealings with Alicia for whom Silva begs Cova's pity. Don Clemente is also a personification of the unconscious, symbolizing the self, or the nucleus of the psyche, whose properties are knowledge, wisdom, insight, and a wish to give advice (*4*, p. 475). Apart from his qualities as a guide and father-figure to Cova, he preaches compassion to his fellow-workers, and charity and forgiveness for Alicia (216). This wise old man is a symbol of the psychic depths, which are nature. As a man of the forest, as a guide, as a cauchero who knows intimately the labyrinths of the jungle and as a compassionate human being, Clemente Silva, as his name suggests, personifies this archetype of the wise old man. It is with the help of Silva that Cova not only pardons Alicia, but is reunited with her, having come to recognize his lack of judgement, and through her meets the monster who has captured her. When the hero has slain the monster-dragon, thereby removing the obstacle, and is reconciled with his princess/ideal woman, the baby is born, thus beginning the regeneration process. For many, if not for Seymour Menton, in his pessimistic Christian interpretation of the novel, birth is a sign of redemption. On several levels (socio-economic, political, even patriotic) Cova has achieved his end. On another level, as I shall demonstrate in Chapter 5, the ideal which he carries within him has found its correspondence in the acceptance of Alicia as his long-sought-after woman. Thus, and most importantly for the Jungian view, the birth of his son and reunion of the hero with his ideal princess is the beneficent result of a search which has liberated the anima, the creative feminine element, from the unconscious.

To all intents and purposes from a Jungian perspective like

Callan's, the novel ends, or should end, at this point, in terms of Rivera's artistic manifestation of the anima/Great Mother conflict and the theme of psychic renewal. Some critics, however, including Callan, find the ending forced and contrived, as if, having brought the hero and his princess together, Rivera was anxious to finish off the novel quickly. For a successful Jungian conclusion, the novel might better have ended with the reconciliation. Since Rivera chose to append an Epilogue which appears to undo some of Callan's theories just expounded, one cannot ignore it or treat it just as a minor inconvenience. The triumph of the jungle over man (the most obvious interpretation of *La vorágine*'s ending), which is a common theme of telluric fiction – as in Horacio Quiroga's short stories, or Graça Aranha's Brazilian novel, *Canãa* (1902) – would seem to Callan and others less convincing, given Clemente Silva's specific role in the novel as the wise old man/guide who has succeeded in the almost impossible task of tracking down his son's bones in the depths of the Amazonian jungle. If one were to pursue the Jungian interpretation beyond the reunion of hero and princess, and identify the fate of Cova with the life and mind of his creator, Rivera, the conclusion is ominous. Quoting Jung, Callan explains: 'Experience shows that the unknown approach of death casts an *adumbratio* (an anticipatory shadow) over the life and dreams of the victim' (*4*, p. 475). By removing his autobiographical protagonist (as some would describe Cova), the author has left some disturbing questions unanswered for his future critics, if not for his contemporaries who were to mourn only four years later his untimely death in New York.

One could argue, of course, to justify the implications of the un-narrated events taking place off-stage before the presentation of the brief, grim Epilogue, that since Cova was swallowed up by the selva of the Terrible Mother of nature, the monster which one assumed he has killed in Barrera, the hero was not successful in the dragon-fight. Even Callan is prepared to concede this interpretation – albeit in a small footnote. Quoting Neumann, Callan admits: 'Time and again, the failure of the dragon-fight . . . proves to be the central problem for neurotics during the first half of life, and the cause of their inability to establish relations with a partner' (*4*, p. 476). By tacking on a disillusionary Epilogue, thus negating the successful completion of the psychic renewal process, Rivera supplies (unconsciously?) the

concluding ironic epitaph to discourage any optimistic interpretations of his novel − in keeping with the eternal struggle in his own
mind and his own life (even in the four years after the publication of
La vorágine) between the search for ideals and the reality that he
found, as I shall show in Chapter 5. Having gone through the process
of exposing his protagonist-hero to the exercise in psychic renewal
and regeneration, rather than concluding the quest myth with the
traditional dragon-fight and the hero-princess reunion, Rivera's metaphysical perspective, his existential pessimism,would not allow him
to end the novel in a patently optimistic way. What may appear to
some to be a betrayal of his aesthetic principles, in terms of structure and composition − I shall argue against this view in Chapter 6
−may well be a more authentic and satisfactory ending in terms of
his philosophical outlook, and more in keeping with his psychological state, no matter how much that may appear to destroy a neat
Jungian conclusion.

This is, of course, not to denigrate Richard Callan's thesis, which
is ingeniously thought out, convincingly argued (on the whole), and
well written. The important point from the Jungian stance is that in
La vorágine Rivera presents an archetypal pattern, as Callan has skilfully demonstrated, which elicits a corresponding archetypal reaction from the reader. Through these responses the interested and intelligent reader participates, perhaps unknowingly, perhaps unwill-
ingly, but nonetheless actively, in the process of psychic renewal, redemption and rebirth. Rivera would not have intended this, nor
would he knowingly have written a Jungian novel − ridiculous as the
statement may sound today − as some modern writers have done
(cf. Robertson Davies' Deptford trilogy, *Fifth Business*, *The Manti-
core*, *World of Wonders*). But Rivera's motives are not important
since, to use the Jungian terminology, the creative function is the
property of the anima, and emanates from the unconscious. As Jung
says: 'Whenever the creative force predominates, human life is ruled
and moulded by the unconscious as against the active will.' In the
artist the Collective Unconscious takes precedence over the personal
in such a way that the artist becomes, or should become, a mere vehicle, a medium for the Collective Unconscious: 'The artist is not a
person endowed with free will who seeks his own ends, but one who
allows art to realize its purpose through him' (*4*, p. 476).

It is less important that one accepts the Jungian interpretation of the novel than that one is prepared to admit that the archetypal patterns of the rebirth drama provide not only a vehicle for fictive discourse but yet another possible approach to the reading of *La vorágine*. In our discussion of the novel and its various planes we have bandied names around from Dante, Ariosto and Cervantes, backward to Homer and Virgil, forward to Freud and Jung, implying that above or below a mythological, theological, biblical, psychological stratum exists another stratum, equally valid as a basis for discussion. Each of these planes provides a path, or a direction, along which one can proceed towards a fruitful reading of a complex, multi-layered novel. It is not necessary that we accept any or all of these interpretations as the meaning of the novel. The important thing for the true work of art is that it can be read, interpreted and appreciated at any or all of these levels. By placing *La vorágine* alongside the *Odyssey*, or the *Aeneid*, or the *Divine Comedy*, or any other great work of art, we are stating explicitly that like the Bible and the myths of old, and through the portrayal of archetypal types of all times, it, as a Colombian novel capable of being studied and enjoyed on various planes, transcends narrow geographical and chronological frontiers.

5 Search for Ideals

In the previous chapter, through a Jungian interpretation, and within the terms of the quest myth, we dealt with *La vorágine* as a manifestation of the search for ideal love, and with Alicia's role as a carrier of Arturo Cova's anima as it attempts to escape from the Great Unconscious. In pre-Jungian terms this phenomenon would be, and still is, regarded as yet another expression of the Romantic tendency to idealize woman.

While I have been careful throughout not to confuse fiction with biography, it is nonetheless a telling point that Rivera put much of himself and his own experiences (consciously or not) into his fictional creation. Nevertheless, Arturo Cova is not Rivera, although one might have difficulty in persuading otherwise some scholars who read *La vorágine* side by side with Neale-Silva's biography. What one can state, however, is that Cova does reflect the dreams, the desires, the illusions of his creator.

The desire for ideal love and the perfect woman is only one manifestation of the search for absolute values which plagues Cova from the first page of the novel (and long before that, as the narrative reveals) – and Rivera from the earliest days of his life and of his literary career. Any amateur psychiatrist will discover in the close bond which united Rivera to his mother the seed of his search for his feminine ideal. This illusory and elusive love was to stay with him for the rest of his life, prompting many outbursts of affection and verse, e.g. 'Gloria'.

This search for love and happiness was a constant in his life and verse, as we see in poems like 'Canto de nupcias' and 'El éxtasis' – 'Yo soy aquel espíritu inconforme/ que, ávido de infinito, en los regazos/ se aturdió de placer, sin que su enorme/ aspiración cupiera en otros brazos,/ siempre triste, insaciable e multiforme' (quoted in *21*, p. 171). This one stanza of 'Canto de nupcias' gives some idea of his attitude to love, only one of the several manifestations of his unslaked thirst for perfection, infinity and unattainable ideal, in which illusion clashes constantly with the harrowing reality of the human condition. Whatever the reasons, and whatever the motives, Rivera was never able to have a full and lasting relationship with a woman — perhaps partly because of his desire for perfection and his Romantic fantasies about the ideal woman, and, not least, from deep-seated psychological reasons rooted, it seems, in the emotional bond with his mother, and also from his own egocentric nature which necessitated that he emerge victorious in any struggle for love. The end result in human and poetic terms was the Romantic aspiration for an unreachable, vague, mysterious beloved, whilst the hard reality was a series of unfulfilled love affairs, symptomatic of his general existential unhappiness (cf. Sonnet XXI in *Tierra de promisión*, Part 3). Since his lack of success in love was but the reflection of an overall attitude to life, it is no wonder that on the path to glory which he followed his desire for perfection took other forms, equally condemned to failure, based as they were on illusions. When hope inevitably led to deception, his 'vanity of vanities' perception of life was merely confirmed.

Although Rivera was influenced by the Modernista movement in his view of poetry (concern for aesthetics, formal debts, etc.), he owed much of his sensibility to the Romantics — and, of course, the *angustia* of the Modernist masters has a similar Romantic ancestry. Although some critics might label Rivera an 'arielista', because his idealism appears to reflect something of the philosophy of the Uruguayan thinker, José Enrique Rodó (1872-1917), Rivera was different from other contemporaries in that his idealism was not rooted in optimism and tended to yield to pessimism in the face of the harsh realities of twentieth-century politics, with which he did try to become involved, unlike most of his Modernist mentors. Confronted with the realization that the Promised Land was but a myth, he tended to retreat into the personal world of his own values, to prepare himself for the next confrontation with reality. He did seek to come to terms with the world around him on several planes, being astute enough to recognize that he had to do so in order to fulfil his dreams — hence his conscious effort to accept the hard facts of the need for money, and a proper job (in politics, in law, in government, in the publishing business). A strange mixture of escapism and activism, dreamer and creator ('un soñador de construcciones y un con-

structor de sueños', *21*, p. 468), Rivera tried to rise above the medi-
ocre and the mundane, the prosaic and the humdrum, an aspiration
which was eventually to lead to his undoing, since he never really
learned to compromise, to accept the conventional, pragmatic approach, whether in politics, literature, life or love.

The Love Quest

It is this same love which preoccupies his creation Cova from the
first pages of the novel. Although he has known many women, and
has had many lovers, what Cova really aspires to is the divine gift of
ideal love. It would be tedious in the extreme to point out again the
analogies between the man Rivera and the character Cova. My intention here is to examine and illustrate the theme of the search for absolute values in *La vorágine*, and particularly in this part the Romantic aspirations towards an ideal love. If I refer to the biographical
data, it is to illumine the text rather than comment on Rivera's life.
Cova, the narrator, is explicit in his affirmation of these illusions:
'Con todo, ambicionaba el don divino del amor ideal, que me encendiera espiritualmente, para que mi alma destellara en mi cuerpo
como la llama sobre el leño que la alimenta' (11). Although we have
looked at the search for ideal love in Jungian terms in the previous
chapter, and examined in some detail the psychological evolution of
Cova (in Chapter 3), one is always tempted to insert enlightening little examples of psychological import into the analysis of Cova's
statements and actions (based on one's knowledge of Rivera's own
tormented life). Cova's affirmation ('Más que el enamorado, fui
siempre el dominador cuyos labios no conocieron la súplica', 11)
certainly constitutes an obstacle towards the realization of his
dreams of attaining ideal love. It also might represent an unconscious
confession of Rivera's own selfishness in love which militates against
any equal sharing or mutual surrender in the things of the heart.
Cova's admission is, of course, yet another example of narcissism,
the vice symbolized by his enemy (and negative alter ego?), Narciso
Barrera. So early in the novel Alicia is still the 'amorío fácil' about
whom he has certain twinges of regret, because he knows that not
only has he deceived her, but he has deceived himself, since Alicia is
merely a sacrifice to his own passions. She cannot be the personifica-

tion of his dreams — at least not yet, the reader adds with hindsight — because one does not find such ideals by searching for them. Cova has practised self-deception by attributing to her qualities that he has never found in any other woman before. He may have dominated her body, but he has not found the spiritual union that he has long desired.

The tragedy for Cova (as for Rivera) is that he never will, because in an important moment of self-confrontation and self-illumination he admits that the search is futile, for there is no solution to it: 'y ya sabías que el ideal no se busca; lo lleva uno consigo mismo' (12). Alicia, a mere sexual possession, cannot hope to take the place of the perfect female figure on the pedestal, whose image he carries deep and irretrievably inside him: ' . . . te hallas, espiritualmente, tan lejos de ella como la constelación taciturna que ya se inclina sobre el horizonte' (12). With poetic language and figures reminiscent of the Romantic sonnets of *Tierra de promisión* ('Purifico mis aguas esperando una estrella/ que vendrá de los cielos a bogar en mis ondas'), Cova sketches the basic problem of idealized love as it clashes with the reality of everyday physical relationships:

> Por todas partes fui buscando en qué distraer mi inconformidad, e iba de buena fe, anheloso de renovar mi vida y de rescatarme a la perversión; pero dondequiera que puse mi esperanza hallé lamentable vacío, embellecido por la fantasía y repudiado por el desencanto. Y así, engañándome con mi propia verdad, logré conocer todas las pasiones y sufro su hastío, y prosigo desorientado, caricatureando el ideal para sugestionarme con el pensamiento de que estoy cercano a la redención. La quimera que persigo es humana, bien sé que de ella parten los caminos para el triunfo, para el bienestar y para el amor . . . ¡Hoy me ha visto usted llorar, no por flaqueza de ánimo, que bastante rencor le tengo a la vida; *lloré por mis aspiraciones engañadas, por mis ensueños desvanecidos, por lo que no fui, por lo que ya no seré jamás*! (24, my italics)

It should be pointed out again that this aspiration to ideal love is only one aspect of a total schema of absolute values stemming from a general search for glory, perfection, renown in various fields, over which Cova agonizes at the outset of the narrative in the first of the self-analytical passages: '¿Y tus sueños de gloria, y tus ansias de triunfo y tus primicias de celebridad?' (12). As Rivera too was to find in his own life, the path to glory is fraught with insurmountable obstacles. Any triumph is perforce transitory, since glory, like the ideal woman, is unattainable.

Given the non-existence of the perfect woman, Cova, in the face of Alicia's aloofness and distancing, initiates, as we saw in Chapter 3, the interesting process of attributing to this ordinary girl the desirable qualities of the ideal woman. Compared to the other women, like la niña Griselda who tempts him, Alicia is obviously different. Cova, who has had no scruples about casual love affairs in the past (by his own admission), resists the temptation not only out of loyalty to his friend Fidel Franco, but also because he is vaguely aware that '... en el fondo de mi determinación corría una idea mentora' (42). In the face of Alicia's indifference and disdain, his feelings towards her are beginning to change. Mere passion is giving way to the initial stages of a new and important process. Alicia, the 'amorío fácil', is becoming in Cova's eyes the ideal woman: 'Desde entonces comencé a apasionarme por ella y hasta me dio por idealizarla' (42). This is not an easy experience for Cova, however, especially when Alicia disappears (willingly, Cova wrongly assumes) with Barrera, provoking yet another spiritual crisis in the protagonist, another outburst of forced criticism against the woman who causes him such pain and suffering (101). The poet soothes his feelings in a wave of sadness and Romantic emotion. If only he had someone to share this beauty! Why should he live alone with art and love?: 'Con humillada pena advertí luego que en el velo de mi ilusión se embozaba Alicia ...' (105). This revelation provokes further efforts by the negative side of the hero to stain the memory of the growing image of the idealized woman. When the lascivious Indian women provoke him with their sexual charms and advances, his chaste reaction (109) might seem out of character, were it not for the psychological change in progress (cf. the crystallization theory of Chapter 3, and the Jungian explanation of Chapter 4).

It is no coincidence that in the character of Cova's good alter ego, Esteban Ramírez, the same illusions towards life and love should be present — illusions which have brought Ramírez to disaster. If he cannot have his ideal woman, at least he can try to preserve his illusions: '¿Pero qué hacer? ¡En esa doncella se detuvo mi aspiración!' (207). Thwarted in love, blinded by fate, lost in the jungle, Ramírez still has his dreams about the 'beldad de categoría' which was denied to him by society and destiny: 'Claro que ella posee virtudes para ser la esposa ideal de que nos habla el Evangelio.' But he is quick to add the qualifying conclusion: 'pero unida a un hombre que no la pervirtiera y encanallara' (208). Accepting failure and defeat as the final reality, Ramírez, rather than try to escape with Cova, prefers the oblivion of the jungle. Thus Cova's alter ego bids farewell to the realization of his dreams, his youth, and the possibility of ever attaining ideal love in the flesh (242). For those who tend to read *La vorágine* in the light of the Cova/Rivera analogy, the powerful episode of Ramírez's disillusionment should provide not only food for thought but a good example of the blurring fusion of characterization which negates a simple autobiographical interpretation of a complex novel.

If Alicia's good qualities are highlighted by her comparison with la niña Griselda, the other camp-followers, and the promiscuous Indian women, the contrast is underscored unequivocally in the description of Cova's amorous adventures with the Turkish man-eater, Zoraida Ayram, who is crude, demanding, and exhausting in her sexual needs. His loathing for la Madona's mercenary excesses prompts Cova to evoke memories and dreams of a different kind of love: 'Hoy, como nunca, siento nostalgia de la mujer ideal y pura, cuyos brazos brinden serenidad para la inquietud, frescura para el ardor, olvido para los vicios y las pasiones. Hoy, como nunca, añoro lo que perdí en tantas doncellas ilusionadas que me miraron con simpatía y que en el secreto de su pudor halagaron la idea de hacerme feliz' (225-26). Not yet quite prepared to admit that Alicia has attained the status of the perfect woman, Cova's mind evokes the memory of the ideal woman in the abstract, then in plural examples, before finally arriving at the case of 'la misma Alicia ... ¡Cuánta diferencia entre ella y la turca, a quien vence en todo, en gracia como en juventud!' (226). When he finally meets Alicia again, after eliminating Barrera whom he needs to kill in order to satisfy the conditions not only of the quest myth but also the idealization process, the reunion brings confirmation of her pregnancy, over which he had agonized earlier in the novel (117). If not exactly willing to grant her ideal

status, he does recognize that she is a good woman whom he almost
lost once, and whom he will now save to share his life.

Thus, in a clear affirmation of the difference between the selfish,
egocentric sexual acts of la Madona, and the unselfish, virtuous love
of Alicia, Cova realizes the desirability and the utility of the married
state and the dignity of parenthood. Alicia has emerged from the
role of casual partner of the opening pages to become a life-giving
woman, and a symbol of the positive aspects of real life, since she
cannot fully become a physical incarnation of an illusion, of an ideal
that exists only in Cova's mind.

The fact that he should rashly and immaturely exhibit the horrif-
ic corpse of his rival to Alicia, and thus bring about the premature
birth of his son, in no way detracts from his confrontation with the
reality/idealism dichotomy in his perception of love. The fact also
that he is willing at the end of the novel to forego his social-redeemer role by refusing, albeit reluctantly, to help the poor lepers, underscores the pragmatic attitude which he has adopted towards his wife
and son. Cova, it appears, has finally learned to distinguish between
dreams and actuality. Whilst recognizing the urge to be a noble pat-
riot and a saviour of mankind, Cova settles for something more
modest, and more within his grasp, the protection of his family
(248). These acts of Cova in the final pages of the novel in no way
reduce the socio-political aspect of the search for values throughout
the novel, since Cova, through the written report bequeathed to
Clemente Silva, has left for posterity a history of the crimes — and
his own attempts to help his fellow-men.

Cova's action, because of his over-zealous protection of his wife
and child, in departing from the hut to escape contamination by the
lepers who had disembarked from their death-ship, is logical and
credible in fictional terms, despite the complaints of some critics
(see Chapter 4). The fact that Clemente Silva, the spirit-guide of the
forest, cannot locate them, even though they are only half an hour
from camp, is more troublesome for the credulity of some critics.
Whether it is technically, artistically or psychologically satisfying or
not, Rivera chose to end the novel thus. In the presentation of Callan's Jungian interpretation in Chapter 4, I tried to suggest possible
explanations for Rivera's apparently flawed ending.

In Seymour Menton's Christian interpretation, Cova is punished for aspiring to ideal love, the property of (the) God(s). That fate, however, is surely more applicable to his 'amigo mental', Ramírez, as I have already suggested. Since Cova comes to terms with his 'ansia de perfección' and accepts something less than ideal love which he sees as clearly out of his reach, the ending may then be seen as Rivera's unconscious punishment of Cova for having betrayed the ideal, for having chosen a flesh-and-blood person in the lack of the mysterious someone who inhabited his poetry and tortured his mind. Cova, then, one might say, was punished, not for aspiring to ideal love but for choosing something inferior, earthly happiness, or at least domestic contentment, which did not figure as a lasting quality in the spiritual vocabulary of Rivera. If Cova compromised his infinite values in return for something more ephemeral, Rivera was not able to make this adjustment in his own constant search for glory in all aspects of his life, whether in love, literature or politics, governed as he was by the code of perfectibility.

The Socio-Political Ideals

The political crisis which has affected Colombia most was the loss of Panama at the beginning of the century. As a youth Rivera lived through this crisis in a family and a region which were politically conscious and sensitive. He also grew up during the *quinquenio* (1904-09) of General Reyes, accused of selling out to foreign investors. Reyes's resignation began a new epoch in Colombian politics, 'la Generación del Centenario', in which Rivera played an active part. As early as 1910, attracted by two different poles, his political ideas were being formed — by stories of the border disputes in the Amazon region especially between Colombia and Peru, and at the same time by the new ideas (socialism, trade unionism, etc.) which were being brought into Colombia by immigrant workers from Europe. Rivera arrived at the conclusion that there was a serious need for social and political reform at all levels. *La vorágine* represents the conscious literary manifestation of this desire for reform. Like his contemporaries of the post-13 March Centenario generation, the young Rivera recognized the necessity for action (part of the dreamer/constructor paradox), but unlike many of his generation he was not against Liberal-Conservative alliances in time of national emergency like the 1914-18 war and the proposed treaty with the U.S.A. to heal the wounds of the Panama secession. In this sense, Rivera's patriotism superseded any party allegiances. When his political involvement, like his legal adventures, failed, Rivera sought the path of glory by operating through diplomatic channels, on his appointment by Gómez Restrepo to be secretary of a mission to Peru and Mexico. But this search for success in diplomatic circles was fated to have the same consequences as the quest for an ideal love, and for the same reasons. The reverses which he suffered on the trip to Peru and Mexico merely confirmed the gap which existed between his illusions and reality – fictionalized once again, and herein lies the importance for us, in the 'sueños irrealizados y triunfos perdidos' of Arturo Cova. How often he was to recognize bitterly that his patriotic ideal in politics and diplomacy was worthless, when faced with the reality of life – hence his growing pessimism. But his disillusionment never quite destroyed his quintessential love of his country.

However, when all else failed for Rivera, he still had recourse to the vehicle that he knew best, literature, in order to voice his protest, in a work that has been variously labelled and criticized, but always praised as a patriotic novel, even by his contemporaries. Being a work of art, of course, *La vorágine* will transcend the merely political and regional level, as I have insisted throughout this study, just as Rivera himself recognized his search for something deeper, in the quest for the elusive ideal, as he confessed to Horacio Franco: 'La urdimbre de la gloria y de la fama es siempre un tejido de patria universalizable y engrandecida por el esfuerzo de la mente y del corazón' (*21*, p. 369). If *La vorágine* is a patriotic novel, then, *colombianidad* has many forms and many levels, like the novel itself. The search for the ideal on the political plane is but one dimension of Rivera's patriotism, just as the novel as a document of social protest reflects only one aspect of *La vorágine*, or one level on which to judge the quest of the protagonist, Arturo Cova. Proud of his patriotism, Rivera, a temporary exile at the end of his life in New York, saw the salutary power of nationalism not as a limiting or narrowing force but as a fertile component of a broader scheme: 'Ligarse a la patria es vincularse al universo y a la vida, porque el suelo donde vimos la luz forma parte de nuestro destino' (*21*, p. 436).

When it came to the business of living, first in love and now in politics, Rivera, like his creation Cova, sought to be free from the boundaries of the human horizon. The social and political dimensions of Cova's escapades in the jungles of the Amazon are but an extension of his ideal quest, his 'afán de perfección', all inextricably bound up with the other manifestations of the search for absolute values (love, literature). His patriotism, one might say, is the abstract, spiritual, pure reflection of something more mundane, more down-to-earth, more realistic — the social and political problems of his day. Thus Cova the poet is more at ease with his adopted role of social redeemer, knight-errant, rescuing maidens in distress, and defending the poor and the humble. Rivera may want to change his country and reform the socio-political system by writing *La vorágine*, but Cova is also tilting at windmills, taking on gigantic enemies, and righting individual wrongs, thus reflecting the idealistic side of Rivera — hence the tendency of some critics to highlight, often in a forced, but understandable, manner, the quixotic nature not only of Cova, but of the novel itself *(13)* — the supreme compliment to *La vorágine* as a universal work of fiction.

Cova is, of course, as we have seen, impulsive, and, as the novel progresses, becomes self-confessedly more unbalanced. Now his motives for fleeing with Alicia, a girl whom he did not even love, may seem flimsy at first glance — to spite her parents who want to marry her off to an older man. The clue in the first lines of the novel, when Cova juxtaposes Violence and Love, putting violence before love in an eye-catching opener, becomes even clearer on the second page, in the brief key passage of self-analysis and self-doubt, which reveals not only his preoccupation with the ideal in terms of love, but something deeper — all his concerns about life, its metaphysical uncertainties, and his anguish in the face of the mystery of existence: '¿Qué has hecho de tu propio destino? .... ¿Y tus sueños de gloria, y tus ansias de triunfo y tus primicias de celebridad?' (12). Apart from the dramatic opening (violence/love), the poet Cova paints the natural background for his self-questioning outburst with a touch reminiscent of his Modernist masters: 'Un silencio infinito flotaba en el ámbito, azulando la transparencia del aire' (12). My aim here, however, is not to portray the literary goals of Cova — I shall leave that aspect of the novel to the next section of this chapter. What I am suggesting is that the flight of Cova, the Modernist artist, is a gesture of dissatisfaction and discontent with the prevailing mores, values and trends in contemporary society. It is also, as Randolph Pope has pointed out, a gesture of defiance against the three pillars of society, the family, religion and the law (*25*, p. 258). The fact that his alter ego, Esteban Ramírez, fled from the same social environment for reasons of ideal love reinforces Cova's point.

In the light of the above, within the framework of his dreams of glory, triumph and fame, Cova views Bogotá (to reverse the order of Seymour Menton's Dantean geographical structure of Chapter 4), as a Hell, as an impediment to attaining his ideal. That Cova should have fled Bogotá is perhaps less satisfactory as a psychological motive or a literary technique than as an indication not only of the ills of the newly-mechanized metropolis but also of the prevailing philistinism and the hypocrisy of the social and moral values of the government elite, the conventional middle classes, and the amorphous masses, who seem to permit and condone through ignorance and apathy the deceptions practised in the name of politics and commerce. For a man like Cova (and Rivera) to whom principles and convictions mean more than platitudes and party loyalties, Bogotá society is anathema. It is no coincidence either that Rivera, each time that he experienced a setback in the face of political reality, should retreat from the city to seek consolation in his beloved nature, in his *patria chica* – or even to the less comfortable regions of the barbarous jungle lands which also fascinated him. Rather than a motiveless pretext, then, Cova's escape from the political and social malaise of the city makes sense, is a logical action in keeping with the protagonist's character, and is an integral part of his idealistic view of life, complete with dreams and illusions.

On the socio-political level, as I illustrated in Chapter 2, Cova's trek through the jungle after Alicia and her abductor takes on greater meaning as a manifestation of his desire not only to rid himself of a rival, but to purge the country of such evil men who exploit his compatriots and besmirch the good name of Colombia. Barrera, El Cayeno, la Madona, and especially Funes, must be destroyed not only for themselves but for the evil system which they represent. The other side of the coin for the author is the government in Bogotá, which allows, even connives at, these abuses, either by silence or by consent, and Rivera's unsuccessful efforts to solve the problems

— hence his disillusionment. In the treatment of the political ideal and the theme of patriotism, Rivera has skilfully shared the narrative voice between Cova and Silva, at times placing the revelations in the mouth of the kindly old guide, rather than entrusting them totally to the perhaps unreliable narrator-protagonist. Just as Esteban Ramírez is presented as the voice of punished ideal love, the political paradise lost is also depicted through the figure of Clemente Silva — both examples of skilful techniques seldom credited to Rivera. When Clemente Silva chastises his fellow-sufferer Balbino Jácome for having co-operated with rubber magnates, his cruellest words are reserved for the Colombian's having betrayed his country and discredited his compatriots. The honour of the fatherland, as Rivera felt, lay in the honesty and ethical standards of the individual citizens, and it was only in the co-operation of all the people for the common good that the republic would prosper, not only materially, but spiritually and morally.

Rivera was very sensitive to the concept of national frontiers and political sovereignty ('patriotismo político-jurídico') — hence his tendency in the novel to point out, through the words of his narrators, the nationality of the exploiters (Venezuelan, Peruvian, Argentine, etc.). But the greatest shame is that of the traitorous Colombians. Despite Clemente Silva's herculean efforts to find his son, and the importance of this search for his personal honour, Silva is prepared to forego freedom and possible reunion with Lucianito in order to report the abuses to the Colombian consul (163). Notwithstanding the irony that his son is in fact already dead, Silva is willing to die for the welfare and the good name of his country. In what could be a summary of Rivera's own efforts as a result of his jungle investigations, Cova ponders his plans:

> ir al Consulado de mi país, exigirle al cónsul que me asesorara en la Prefectura o en el Juzgado, denunciar los crímenes de la selva, referir cuanto me constaba sobre la expedición del sabio francés, solicitar mi repatriación, la libertad de los caucheros esclavizados, la revisión de libros y cuentas en La Chorrera y en El Encanto, la redención de miles de indígenas, el amparo de los colonos, el libre comercio en caños y ríos. (164).

Those critics who condemn Clemente Silva's story as a digression, which detracts from the unity of the novel, have not perceived the importance of this thread of the patriotic novel in *La vorágine*. When Don Clemente does find the consul, he is disheartened, ashamed and angry to find that the consul is not even a Colombian, nor does he care about Colombia — his only connection with the beloved fatherland is that he sells passports. The ultimate humiliation comes when Silva asks that arrangements be made to send him back home, only to be told: 'Su país no repatria a nadie. El pasaporte vale cincuenta soles' (167). So much for patriotic honour and the reputation of the republic. Rivera ends the important Part 2 and Clemente Silva's narrative by finally announcing the alleged death of Silva's long-lost son (168). With the apparent death of Lucianito, Clemente's illusions die with him, since he had devoted the greater part of his life searching for this son. Within the framework of the patriotic novel, this symbolic death, following closely on Silva's disillusionment with the consul, the visitador, the judge and other Colombian officials, underscores the reality of life compared to the patriotic ideals of Cova and Silva.

In the opening scene of Part 3, in the ambiguous song of the cauchero, the voices of Clemente Silva and Arturo Cova are fused in the *cri de coeur* '¡Yo he sido cauchero, yo soy cauchero!'. By means of this technique of confusion, which Rivera uses occasionally in the novel (cf. 179), he juxtaposes the words of Silva and Cova as Cova narrates the litany of his sufferings, and puts himself in the old man's place, thus becoming, in reverse, the spokesman for Clemente, and all the other hopeless slaves, not only of the jungle but of life itself, who will never realize their dreams:

> ¿Quién estableció el desequilibrio entre la realidad y el alma incolmable? ¿Para qué nos dieron alas en el vacío? ¡Nuestra madrastra fue la pobreza, nuestro tirano la aspiración! Por mirar la altura tropezábamos en la tierra; por atender al vientre misérrimo fracasamos en el espíritu. La medianía nos brindó su angustia. ¡Sólo fuimos los héroes de lo mediocre! (169)

In this, one of the most poignant passages in the novel, Cova raises his cry beyond a personal outpouring of his disillusionment and despair (cf. Martín Fierro as a similar gaucho-Everyman), and certainly reflects the disappointment with life of his creator:

> ¡El que logró entrever la vida feliz no ha tenido con qué comprarla; el que buscó la novia, halló el desdén; el que soñó con la esposa, encontró la querida, el que intentó elevarse, cayó vencido, ante los magnates indiferentes, tan impasibles como estos árboles que nos miran languidecer de fiebres y de hambre entre sanguijuelas y hormigas! (169)

In this pessimistic but stoic description of his own aspirations, with regard to his own life and relations with Alicia and the rubber bosses, Cova rises to embrace all men in their unattainable search for something higher: '¡Quise hacerle descuentos a la ilusión, pero incógnita fuerza disparóme más allá de la realidad! ¡Pasé por encima de la ventura, como flecha que marra su blanco, sin poder corregir el fatal impulso y sin otro destino que caer! ¡Y a esto lo llamaban mi *porvenir*!' (169-70). In his regret for things that might have been, Cova's unfulfilled dreams and lost triumphs come back to haunt his memory like ghosts, as if they wanted to remind him constantly of his shame for not having achieved his desires and his ambitions.

This apologia of the caucheros is a very moving hymn. It is also a very complex passage technically, in that it makes use of the double voice of Cova and Clemente to portray the sufferings of Cova, of the caucheros in particular, and of all mankind in general. Also, in a fine display of ambivalence, it laments the crimes committed against the jungle by these same caucheros, imbued with the mad desire to make a quick fortune. The aim is riches and glory; the reality is fever, lice and ants. In the knowledge that their dreams are not going to be realized, and that they are not going to reach that fabled and symbolic other shore ('la playa opuesta, a donde nunca lograremos ir', 170), the narrator, in an outburst of desperate, Lucifer-like protest against the exploiters and fate, vows to raise the struggle to cosmic heights and to die proudly for a just cause: '¡Quisiera librar la batalla de las especies, morir en los cataclismos, ver invertidas las fuerzas cósmicas! ¡Si Satán dirigiera esta rebelión . . . !' (171). Thus in a epigrammatic, suggestive way Rivera directs our attention once again to classical, Miltonic, and Romantic sources which elevate Cova to a position above and beyond the rebellious and disillusioned cauchero, and the novel to universal heights superior to the mere patriotic novel of social protest. Cova's role in the novel is changed as a result of this conscious decision — he is now an avenging angel of destruction. If his downtrodden compatriots see him as a saviour or a social redeemer, he will grow into that role too, killing the exploiters (Barrera, El Cayeno) and destroying the system (Funes), even if it means using the instruments of the system (la Madona) to achieve his ends: '... soy por idiosincrasia el amigo de los débiles y de los tristes' (136).

The fact that his friend and good alter ego Esteban Ramírez also suffers at the hands of the social exploiters underscores the political message of the novel. As a witness of Funes' terrible massacre at San Fernando, the blind Ramírez describes the horrible events to Cova who is eager to hear. Ironically, the sightless Esteban becomes the eyes of Cova, who in turn becomes the avenging hand of his friend, not only by writing down the history, but also by striking down the offenders. As a redeemer-figure, Cova performs actions that are not only destructive but positive and constructive, with regard to his people and his country. These poor Colombians have gathered around Cova who becomes a Moses-type figure destined, they hope, to lead them out of the jungle-hell into the Promised Land — the repatriation long sought by Clemente Silva: '¡Vete, pero no olivides que merecemos la redención! ... Nosotros también queremos regresar a nuestras llanuras, también tenemos madre a quien adorar!' (214). But as Clemente Silva found to his sorrow, confirming Cova's disillusionment, Colombia, a country served by alien, ignorant and indifferent functionaries, provides no shelter for its own. The Promised Land is truly a myth, like that of El Dorado and other legendary places.

With the grisly death of the foreign exploiter, El Cayeno, Cova rejoices in his native pride: '¡Así murió aquel extranjero, aquel invasor, que en los lindes patrios taló las selvas, mató los indios, esclavizó a mis compatriotas!' (245). His work as national saviour, however, is not yet complete. Cova leaves a letter for the Colombian consul, invoking his humanitarian sentiments on behalf of his compatriots, 'víctimas del pillaje y la esclavitud, que gimen entre la selva, lejos de hogar y patria' (246), before undertaking his final and most important act on behalf of his country, the killing of Barrera. The struggle is long and silent, the description brief and eloquent: 'Ya libré a mi patria del hijo infame' (247). The fact that Barrera is also the symbolic obstacle between him and his ideal love demonstrates once again Rivera's skill in weaving the various threads of the narrative in a convincing way to its successful conclusion. Reunited with the beloved, Cova no longer needs to play the active part of social saviour, a role which has been an integral unit of his general search for perfection. In the history of his travels and experiences, which he left with Clemente Silva for the consul, his contribution to the fatherland is fully documented. There is a certain irony in Cova's instructions to Silva, as Randolph Pope has also observed (*25*, p. 262), since both Silva and Cova have found through their own experiences that the consul in unwilling and unable to achieve anything for the Colombians. That the protagonist even imagines that things may be different this time is another example of the eternal clash between idealism and reality in Cova's character.

The Literary Goals

From his earliest days in Neiva, literature, like nature, had an important role to play in Rivera's life, in a consoling and formative way. As a child he had read the poems of Zorrilla and Espronceda, Bello and Heredia, which provided a refuge and an inspiration for the early manifestations of his 'ideal de femineidad' and the 'aspiración a la gloria'. At school, university, and throughout his career, literature was not only a means of escape from the anguish of life but, when all else failed, the one source of consolation. And, appropriately, literature was also for Rivera the vehicle which he used to articulate these very failures of his sentimental and political experiences. As such, it became a positive instrument with which to confront the inevitable disillusionment which was a constant of his life. One sees a clear pattern in Rivera's life. When faced with yet another deception or defeat (in politics, love, diplomacy, the law), he turns again to Art as the only constant, and the sympathetic company of fellow-writers. In this sense *La vorágine* is the culminating and lasting tribute to his literary/political/personal search for perfection: 'La perfección ha sido siempre una quimera tras la cual encarna el hombre sus aspiraciones sin que nunca la realidad sepa corresponder a la grandeza del empeño' (*21*, p. 214).

It is significant that Rivera started to write the novel as, at least consciously, a reaction to his inability to persuade his countrymen, politically and diplomatically, of the need for, and the means of achieving, reform in Colombia. This was yet another attempt to present himself as the strong man of action as well as the thinker. In writing he was able to synthesize the 'soñador/constructor' dichotomy which forever waged war in his mind, fusing the poetic ideals of love with the glorious patriotic dreams of doing something concrete and useful for his country He wanted desperately to be taken seriously, and his work not simply to be considered quixotic ('cosas de poeta'), nor merely a political tract. As I suggested in Chapter 2, literature was his vocation. Politics provided the material for his art. When *La vorágine* was attacked by his contemporaries as being inferior to *Tierra de promisión*, he rose violently to his own defence. The foreign praise (by Quiroga, Blasco Ibáñez, Alfonso Reyes and others), however, went a long way to bolstering up his self-esteem as an artist, and indicating the direction that he must follow to fulfil his desire for glory.

The fact that the protagonist-narrator, to whom Rivera delegated the task of articulating in artistic terms the manifestation of the author's own vital sensibility and values, should also be a poet, is, of course, very significant. The implication is that Art is not only the vehicle by which the spiritual quest is transliterated, but becomes the effect itself. That is, literature is not only an aesthetic instrument but a metaphysical tool which helps to give meaning as well as shape to life itself. I have suggested that for Rivera, in the face of legal, political, and sentimental setbacks, literature was the only constant to which he continually had recourse. In Cova's early self-questioning about his dreams of glory and his desire for triumph and fame, the artistic ideal is to the forefront.

In the plains of Casanare, Cova, in a moment of fantasy, imagines himself with Alicia and baby back in the (paradoxically) Promised Land of Bogotá, in the midst of his fellow-students, to whom he would also boast about his newly gained wealth: 'Poco a poco, mis buenos éxitos literarios irían conquistando el indulto' (45). The reverie is interrupted by Don Rafo's admonition to the 'soñador', followed by a toast to the illusory fortune and love. The reality, as Cova is quick to recognize, is pain and death (45). In some beautiful Mod-

ernist passages already quoted, like the dawn scene (20), the poet reveals himself, unwittingly perhaps, preoccupied as he is at this stage
with self-confessed obsessions with riches. Despite the psychological
evolution of the unbalanced Cova in the face of a hostile jungle, the
artist in him appreciates and records the beauty of these natural images in all their detail. In truly Romantic fashion, as poet identifies
with nature, Cova paints the landscape for us with an artist's skill
and terminology: 'Sobre el panorama crepuscular fuese ampliando
mi desconsuelo, como la noche, y lentamente una misma sombra
borró los perfiles del bosque estático, la línea del agua inmóvil, las
siluetas de los remeros . . . ' (98). This could be one of the set-pieces
composed by Rivera on his travels, as his critics are wont to point
out, but it captures perfectly the state of mind of the disillusioned
poet in the natural setting, and prepares the way, along with the
beautiful heron description (104), for the transformation in his mind
of Alicia as 'la mujer querida' (if not yet his ideal woman).

In his changeable, hallucinating mind, under the influence of the
selva and the tales of the legendary Indian spirit, Mapiripama, even
death in its horror is portrayed as beautiful: 'La visión frenética del
naufragio me sacudió con una ráfaga de belleza. El espectáculo fue
magnífico . . . ' (126). Although Silva's story and experiences bring
Cova down to the reality of the protest novel, the political failures
serve merely to underline the unrealized dreams and lost triumphs –
the wealth unobtained and the literary fame lost forever. In a bitter
outburst (176) which is a satiric parody of Modernist poetry, Cova
rejects his past and his poetic ideals in a litany of images (nightin-
gales in love, Versailles gardens, sentimental views), which contrast
starkly with the surrounding reality of rotten trees, dead bees, and
flowers which are obscene in their sexual palpitations.

Although Cova seldom resurrects his poetic ideals throughout the
rest of the novel, dominated as he is by the sole need for survival in
order to kill Barrera and be with Alicia, the object of his desire, the
poetic spirit in him does not die. It lies submerged, and appears, but
fitfully, to paint a jungle scene of fascinating horror. It is also his
poetic instinct which helps him to understand the fatal attraction
which la Madona has over the poor caucheros, and to appreciate the
promise of redemption which her beguiling music speaks to the mis-
erable, the lonely and the helpless:

Lentamente, dentro del perímetro de los ranchos, empezó a flotar una melodía semirreligiosa, leve como el humo de los turíbulos. Tuve la impresión de que una flauta estaba dialogando con las estrellas. Luego me pareció que la noche era más azul y que un coro de monjas cantaba en el seno de las montañas, con acento adelgazado por los follajes, desde inconcebibles lejanías. Era que la madona Zoraida Ayram tocaba sobre sus muslos un acordeón.

Aquella música de secreto y de intimidad daba motivo a evocaciones y a saudades . . . Mi psiquis de poeta, que traduce el idioma de los sonidos, entendió lo que aquella música les iba diciendo a los circunstantes. Hizo a los caucheros una promesa de redención . . . ; consoló a las mujeres esclavizadas . . . , e individualmente nos trajo a todos el don de encariñarnos con nuestras penas por medio del suspiro y de la ensoñación. (201)

Rivera subtly fuses the basic ideals of love, feeling for the homeland, and poetry through the simple haunting melody of the accordion, which conjures up profound feelings of longing in men's hearts, transcending the conventionally religious to reach spiritual or supernatural heights which go beyond fervent patriotism to suggest a deliverance in an even happier Land of Promise. To have achieved thus a felicitous synthesis of the various levels of the novel and Rivera's ideals is no mean artistic feat.

Recognizing that he has not achieved the artistic glory which he craved, nor the literary success that he dreamed about in the Casanare plain, Cova is fated, then, apart from parodying the verses which he once struggled to emulate and depicting in poetic prose the striking features of the hostile landscape, to report for posterity the history of the jungle abuses as they are reflected in the memoirs of his odyssey: 'Peripecias extravagantes, detalles pueriles, páginas truculentas forman la red precaria de mi narración, y la voy exponiendo con pesadumbre al ver que mi vida no conquistó lo trascendental y en ella todo resulta insignificante y perecedero' (216). These self-denigrating childish details and truculent pages, written out of a sense of failure, constitute, ironically, as we shall see in Chapter 6, a manuscript which belies the narrator's feelings of inadequacy and results in something far from insignificant or transitory, as the pessimistic Cova had predicted. In literature, if not in life, Cova the poet has achieved the transcendental glory, the success, and the immortality that he desired – through the magic of art.

In the final pages of *La vorágine* Cova leaves a letter for the Colombian consul in which he renounces his aspirations and confronts the reality of what he is, whilst regretting what he might have been: '... despido de lo que fui, de lo que anhelé, de lo que en otro ambiente pude haber sido' (246). This is almost a perfect echo of his remark in the purported 'Fragmento de la carta de Arturo Cova' which serves as an epigraph or introductory tag to the novel: '... los que al recordarme alguna vez piensen en mi fracaso y se pregunten por qué no fui lo que pude haber sido' (7). That is to say, Cova's narrative is sandwiched between two explicit affirmations of his failure. Rivera, of course, inserted the epigraph after writing the novel, as an unequivocal restatement of the failures, the 'sueños irrealizados' and the 'triunfos perdidos' as they are manifest in the novel, and as a clear reflection of his own state of mind, 'el fracasado anhelo de lo que nunca he sido'.

Rivera's whole life was a search for illusory ideals in love, politics and literature. That he seldom managed to distinguish between his absolute values and real life, preferring to take refuge in the unattainable goals of his inner being, was the root of his existentialist unhappiness. However tragic that might be for the man José Eustasio Rivera, the fact that the novelist was able to take this contrast between 'el continuo devenir' and 'lo que perdura', the flux and the constant, which motivated his eternal but always failing search for glory, and fuse it into a fictional creation, *La vorágine*, represents a lasting tribute to the artist, long after the defects of the man and the inadequacies of the politician are forgotten. His great wish was to give back to the *patria*, which inspired him, the literature which might earn him the coveted title of 'poet of Colombia': 'Sé cuánto me falta, sé a cuánto aspiro. Veinte años más pido a la vida para merecer honradamente el solo título de poeta, cuando pueda decir: "aquí están mis obras, aquí devuelvo a la patria, en arte nacional, lo que de ella recibiera en inspiración" ' (*15*, p. 177). Rivera was not granted his request for two more decades to complete his work. His reputation must rest on a collection of poems and one novel which captures man's unfulfilled search for love and glory, in all its tragic and noble beauty.

6 *Narrative Structure*

One of the main criticisms of *La vorágine* over the years has been that it suffers from a lack of shape, unity, form and organization. Even those critics who praise Rivera's patriotic fervour, his gifts of observation, and his powerful descriptive passages, censure the novel for its serious lack of structure. In the journalistic polemic that he waged with Rivera in 1926, Luis Trigueros condemns the novel out of hand:

> *La vorágine* ... es un caos de sucesos aterrantes, una maraña de escenas inconexas, un confuso laberinto en que los personajes entran y salen, surgen y aparecen sin motivos precisos ni causas justificativas. Falta en ellos, por otra parte, el sentido de la lógica y trabazón espiritual ... Lánguida de acción, flaca de argumento, horra de sutileza y de análisis anímico, *La vorágine* no es casi una novela ... (*El Espectador*, 24 November 1926, repr. in *21*, p. 374)

This is an extreme example of the kind of criticism, some of it prompted by personal and political animosity, used to attack the form and the narrative structure of the novel.

It is obvious that most of Rivera's contemporaries who were hostile to *La vorágine* had great difficulty in coming to terms with its genre, or with the figure of the protagonist in his role as poet and intellectual, as I demonstrated in Chapter 5. If it is read only as a social document, or as an adventure story, or as travel literature, then the narrative thread and the system of narrative voices present difficulties to those who underestimate its structural complexity, seeing it only as disorganized autobiographical fiction. I am not the first to point out the irony of Rivera's technique of having the novel end simultaneously with Cova's manuscript, thus prefiguring the much vaunted ingenious device employed by his compatriot García Márquez in *Cien años de soledad*. Twenty years after the publication of the novel, in what was a pioneer work of criticism on Latin American fiction, Jefferson Rea Spell, whilst praising other aspects of the novel, mainly its realistic description of little-known jungle regions, concludes that *La vorágine*, ' . . . from the standpoint of technique in novel writing, is formless and unintegrated' (*28*, p. 181). This was the general attitude of critics for at least two more decades, concerned as they were then with highlighting the deserved psychological merits of the novel, which hitherto had been neglected in favour of the socio-political and geographical elements of the novel of the land as document. No real breakthrough in the study of *La vorágine* from the perspective of narrative structure appears until the mid- and late 1960s, and even then only sporadically, and with limited reception.

In two articles appearing within a year of each other Joan Green (*14*) and Ernesto Porras Collante (*26*) point the way to the future with structural emphases which highlight for the first time the importance not only of the provocative content, but also of the form, the necessary and perfect fusion of which results in the work of art. Porras, in a work which is rather pretentiously entitled a 'structural interpretation', and at times equally ponderously analysed, labelled and illustrated with figures, tables and the like, does suggest, however, a fruitful approach in his introduction, which coincides with the basis of my discussion of this complex novel: 'Obras como *La vorágine* no entregan su total significación al primer contacto superficial: múltiples y no entrevistos aspectos surgen ante nosotros cuando por procedimientos metódicos remontamos la singularidad de los fenómenos y descubrimos múltiples interrelaciones y mediaciones' (*26*, p. 241). Taking as the point of departure for his 'structural approach' to the novel the well-known basic theories of Wellek and Warren, the interpretation and the analysis of the literary works themselves,[13] Porras recalls the warning to Socrates and his disciples in Plato's *Hippias Major* not to separate and isolate the objects of their study so much that they fail to see the totality of the great continuous reality of things. If Rivera's contemporaries had heeded the warning, *La vorágine* might have been better understood and appreciated by those narrow-minded critics who could not see the forest

[13]René Wellek and Austin Warren, *Theory of Literature* (New York: Harcourt, Brace & World, 1949; 3rd ed., Harmondsworth: Penguin, 1963).

for the trees. Porras's article, although not very valuable in itself, represents a turning point in Rivera criticism. Although he still uses the theories of the (by now traditional) New Critics like Wellek and Warren, and even older ones like E. M. Forster (*Aspects of the Novel*), Porras's passing references to Ferdinand de Saussure's *Cours de linguistique générale* (which has inspired both structuralism and semiotics) and Kurt Baldinger's 'Sémantique et structure conceptuelle' (for discussion of the concept of 'microstructure', 'macrostructure', and 'structure') point the. way perhaps to yet another fruitful stage in *La vorágine* criticism. The delay in developing that stage may be due to Porras's obvious, uninspired, and uninspiring mathematical division of the novel, along with his social-sciences-report style, which, unfortunately, contributes little new to our knowledge or appreciation of the novel — in spite of the promising opening of his epigraph and introduction.

Much more rewarding, though not entirely revolutionary, is Joan Green's attempt not to deal exclusively with the structure of the novel, which often leads to a mere cataloguing and categorization of events, but with the function of the narrator and the narrative mode of *La vorágine*. In previous chapters, when dealing with various aspects of the novel (the social in Chapter 2, the artistic in Chapter 5), I have had occasion perforce to refer to the various narrators, especially the protagonist Cova, Clemente Silva, Helí Mesa, Esteban Ramírez, Balbino Jácome, and their individual roles in the novel. The main narrative voice is by definition that of the protagonist, since the manuscript that we read as the novel purports to be his memoirs. Since Cova is the protagonist and chief narrator, the other characters exist and revolve around him. They depend on him for their existence not only as characters in life as in the novel, but also as narrators. Their narratives exist in the novel because and when Cova invites them to tell their tale, for example, Clemente Silva's long, detailed history of the search for his son, his tribulations in the selva, and the abuses of the *cauchería*. So too with Esteban Ramírez's report of the Funes massacre at San Fernando, which Ramírez (not Cova) had witnessed. In other words, the principal narrator and the other figures are mutually supportive and dependent. If their narrative cannot exist outside Cova's narrative, the reverse is also true. Cova would not be able to describe events and scenes that he personally had not witnessed were it not for the confessions, stories and reports of his friends and companions in distress.

The efficacy of the narrative technique becomes even more marked when the voices of the individual narrators become blurred, fused, even confused (as I pointed out in Chapter 5), for example, in the hymn of the cauchero speech, opening Part 3 (169-71), '¡Yo he sido cauchero, yo soy cauchero!' This apologia may be interpreted in different ways. Clemente Silva, long under the rhetorical influence of Cova, might begin to speak like the narrator, adopting the poetic, epic tone of his muse, to complain of his fate, unfulfilled dreams, and the exploitation of his compatriots, ending with his fist raised to heaven in the defiant challenge to man and God: '¡Yo he sido cauchero, yo soy cauchero! ¡Y lo que hizo mi mano contra los árboles puede hacerlo contra los hombres!' (171). But, of course, this sounds much more like Cova, although he has not been and is not a cauchero. However, on other occasions Cova has taken the words out of Silva's mouth, as it were, assuming not only the identity but the voice and the spoken word of the old guide. Together, by mutual prompting and completing each other's sentences, they narrate the adventures of Clemente Silva and his six lost companions:

—Éramos siete caucheros prófugos.

—Y quisieron matarlo . . .

—Creían que los extraviaba intencionalmente.

—Y unas veces lo maltrataban . . .

—Y otras me pedían de rodillas la salvación.

—Y lo amarraron una noche entera . . .

—Temiendo que pudiera abandonarlos.

—Y se dispersaron por buscar el rumbo . . .

—Pero sólo toparon el de la muerte. (179)

With the fusion of the voices, the narrative thread becomes entangled, producing a double or even multiple effect — the formal reflection of the complicated content, the aesthetic manifestation of the metaphysical complexity of the novel.

Rather than a formless chaotic mass, then, *La vorágine* is a rich, multi-layered, multi-faceted work of art. The fusion of voices and identities and apparent ambiguity (as in the best of the novels of

Vargas Llosa, Carlos Fuentes, José Donoso, for example) offer a rewarding challenge to the accomplice reader who is invited to collab-
orate in the reading/narrating of the novel by distinguishing and
identifying with the different voices and their stories. It is the anti-
thesis/synthesis of the composite voices and narrations which goes to
make up the unusual structure of the novel. In other words, within
the narrative of Arturo Cova, and yet separate from it, exist the narrations of the other characters. It is through Rivera's skilful blending
of the individual stories of the secondary figures into Cova's narrative that the author has produced what I shall call for the moment
the work of fiction *La vorágine*, which readers enjoy today.

   The novelty of Green's approach is to tackle the narrative problem from an angle other than that of the traditional first-person or
third-person omniscient narrator. I should not perhaps stress too
much the originality of Green's focus, since it is firmly based on the
works of two critics, one of whom might be regarded as out-of-date
by today's standards — Wayne C. Booth's *The Rhetoric of Fiction*
(Chicago: University of Chicago Press, 1961) and Percy Lubbock's
The Craft of Fiction (London: Jonathan Cape, 1921). Green's inn-
ovation was to have taken the narrative theories of the aforementioned critics and applied them to a Latin-American novel (in a way
that critics today might use the ideas of Gérard Genette or Mikhail
Bakhtin, for example, to look afresh at the work of Lezama Lima or
Cabrera Infante), with interesting, if not astounding, results.[14] In
this way, Rivera's characters take on new roles, new lights and new
functions. They can be classified, for example, as 'narradores dramatizados', whose characteristics and opinions correspond to those of
the author; or they can be 'observadores' or 'narradores agentes' who
have an effect on the action of the novel, presenting their stories as
dramatized scenes, or a combination of both; or they can be 'narradores disfrazados' who inform the reader, whilst apparently only
playing their own part in the novel (*14*, p. 101). Within this framework, one has to take into account also the question of distance
which separates the narrator from the other characters, from the action, from the author, and from the novel. This distinction can be
temporal, spatial and aesthetic, as well as intellectual and moral (*14*,

---

[14] See, for instance, John Brushwood, *Genteel Barbarism* (Lincoln: University
of Nebraska Press, 1981).

p. 102).

In Chapter 5, in my treatment of Cova as a patriotic social redeemer and searcher for ideals, I stressed the importance of the Prologue and the Epilogue not just as artificial literary bookends which frame the narrative of Cova, but as significant statements from the metaphysical point of view with regard to Cova's illusions and ultimate fate, and as important parts of the literary technique used by Rivera to stress the authenticity of the novel. In this Prologue 'Rivera' the narrator (not to be confused with Rivera the author), purportedly replying to a letter from the Minister, claims to have arranged the papers of Arturo Cova for publication, respecting the style and errors of the poet and underlining only the provincialisms. Does 'arranging' mean that he took the liberty of omitting some parts and thus technically editing the manuscript? If so, his role as a non-dramatized narrator is more ambiguous.

Richard Ford, in a later perceptive article (*10*) dealing with the narrative frame of the novel, raises some interesting questions about narrative technique and the role of the 'editor/Rivera' in arranging the papers. Did the editor paraphrase? Did he faithfully copy it out? Or do we have the original manuscript? (*10*, p. 574). One echoes Ford's questions, because the Prologue has an important role to play in the narrative framework of the novel. Even in the Prologue 'Rivera' promises us at the other end of the frame the Epilogue, which whets the reader's appetite and creates a kind of literary suspense, curious as we are to find out, like 'Rivera', the eventual fate of the protagonist. True to his role in the Prologue, 'Rivera' keeps his distance, coolly, dispassionately announcing a brief telegram which tells all. The other end of the narrative frame confirms the role of 'Rivera' as a reporter whose function is simply to present to us the manuscript/narrative of Arturo Cova. This distancing of the editor 'Rivera' is meant to give an appearance and atmosphere of reality to fiction. It also suggests in a convincing way the independence and self-sufficiency of Cova, and in a sense takes the blame from 'Rivera' who is a mere intermediary, the servant of the Minister. By means of this ingenious technique the direct contact will be between Cova and the reader.

In the second paragraph of the Prologue 'Rivera' suggests to the Minister that the book be not published until all the information about the exploitation of the rubber-workers is available. Skilfully adding to the desired 'truthfulness' of the novel (cf. Chapter 2) and

thus strengthening its value as a work of social protest, the author
Rivera, through the intermediary of the editor 'Rivera', also dis-
tances himself from the manuscript, and thus paradoxically underscores the fictional element by the device of 'finding' and 'arranging'
the papers. In this sense, 'Rivera', the finder and arranger of the papers of Cova, is also a narrator (non-dramatized) by Green's adapta-
tion of Wayne Booth's definition, but not an omniscient narrator,
since he claims not to know at this stage Cova's fate – only until the
point when Cova and Alicia leave the hut to escape contamination
from the lepers. In this sense he is like those characters of Vargas
Llosa (in *La ciudad y los perros*, for example) who are no more
knowledgeable than the readers, since they do not have all the information. There are still surprises in store for 'Rivera' and the reader. 'Rivera' the narrator does not appear again till the last page when
the Epilogue informs us of the cable which he received from the consul giving us the news of Cova's disappearance. As narrator, then,
'Rivera' asks us to accept Cova's narrative as it is, without authorial
intervention or comment (*14*, p. 103). In other words, what we have
in the novel is Cova's view of the situation (jungle abuses, etc.) and
of the world. As a first-person narrative, it should be more authentic,
more believable, more true, more convincing, since there is no third-
person interlocutor telling us what Cova thought or why he behaved
thus. That is to say, it is a subjective narrative, with all the first-hand
virtues (and, one might add, all the limitations) of the protagonist
Arturo Cova. In fact, as Richard Ford shrewdly points out, we know
Cova better than he knows himself, because at the end of the novel
we have all the information from all the narratives, including the
promised all-revealing Epilogue (*10*, p. 573).

As the protagonist, Cova is, of course, the most important narrator. Before we turn our attention to his narrative, however, there is
one other piece of narrative, apart from the Prologue and the Epilogue, which demands our scrutiny. This is the important 'Fragmento de la carta de Arturo Cova' (mentioned in Chapter 5), which pre-
cedes even the Prologue. Ford again asks the right questions (*10*,
p. 574), although he does not have many answers. Who is responsible
for this fragment? And why only a fragment? Did 'Rivera' edit this
from the whole letter? If so, why did he publish it? To give us a fore-
taste of the future narrative? To prepare us for the character of Cova

and his Romantic destiny? Or merely to remember him with a dedicatory epigraph? If so, why have the prologue as well? Whatever the reason, the fragment does serve as a double prologue, prefiguring the Epilogue, gives us an idea of the character of Cova which will become manifest in his own narrative, and serves also as a sample of Cova's literary style. Once again, by an ingenious literary technique, Rivera links metaphysics and aesthetics. But more than a trick, this fragment is an essential component of the underestimated narrative structure of *La vorágine*.

From the hints of the letter-fragment, we have a mental picture of Cova which is fleshed out in his narrative, not only by his description of his and others' actions, the natural setting and the social abuses, but also by the autobiographical picture of his own spiritual and mental life, with all its imbalances from insomnia to hallucination to homicide and suicide. The fact that he is a poet and an artist colours his way of seeing and describing things and events. As I suggested earlier (in Chapter 5), the great irony is that Cova, despite his literary dreams and failures, finally does gain artistic renown − for this manuscript. We do not find out how he feels until near the end of the novel (216), when he first decides to put pen to paper − just before he overtakes Alicia − in the company of his alter ego, Esteban Ramírez. In other words, it is not a day-to-day diary of his experiences, from the time he left Bogotá, through the plains and jungles. Modestly he claims that these notes of his odyssey were written merely as a kind of exemplary narrative for his friend, to describe his past adventures. Thus, Arturo Cova, as an omniscient narrator with hindsight, in the space of six weeks writes a narrative of the events of the past eight months. In this sense the narrative up to page 216 can truly be called memoirs, since he recalls events, and even comments on them, from his temporal and spatial vantage-point of the present (i.e. page 216) in Ramírez's tent. With this privileged information, he can even make use of literary techniques like prefiguration (*10*, p. 576) − for example, he knows that Fidel will set fire to the ranch and that they will both set out in a search for their women. This special knowledge, of course, leads to a certain self-conscious literary posturing on Cova's part up to this point (p. 216), since he knows how the events will have turned out. But this decision to write his memoirs marks the narrative watershed of the novel, since Cova, like 'Rivera' of the Prologue, and the reader, does not know what will happen from this day onwards. In other words, as of page 216 Cova's memoirs cease and his daily diary begins, as his literary style in the present tense indicates — for example, 'Esto lo escribo aquí' (247). When Cova says 'Yo no sé lo que va a pasar' (246), we know that he means it, and that he has no more information than the reader. What was for 216 pages a description or remembrance of past events has become a harrowing, personal, urgent document — not just a report of the massacre of San Fernando, nor merely a journal to instruct or entertain his friend, as he modestly claims.

Ford, in his astute analysis of the structure of the novel, rejects this theory of Cova's writing only for a long-lost friend, whom he had never even mentioned until his surprising entry into the narrative — one of the many cases, by the way, of anagnorisis (the recognition of the true identity of a person) in the novel (*23*, p. 464). As I suggested in Chapter 5, it is rather ironic that Cova should write a manuscript for a friend who is blinded and unable to read. Also, why record Ramírez's report of well-known events, if it is only for his friend and not for other readers? Also, if Ramírez is the only destined reader, why does he warn the other readers that they will never read this: 'Erraría quien imaginara que mi lápiz se mueve con deseos de notoriedad, al correr presuroso en el papel, en seguimiento de las palabras para irlas clavando sobre las líneas' (216). Although he claims to be writing only for Ramírez, there is no doubt that consciously (in which case Cova is a liar) or unconsciously (surely a reflection of his now-known search for literary prestige) there are implied readers other than his spiritual friend. We never know if Ramírez will ever be physically capable of reading it, or if he even wants to. Cova, then, is distancing himself from his readers in the same way that Rivera did by means of the Prologue/Epilogue technique. If we accept that Cova is not deliberately lying (although this is not out of the question, given his unstable condition and previous character flaws), but is only bending the truth, the obvious assumption is that there are other readers beyond Esteban Ramírez. The fact that he does not leave the manuscript with Ramírez on his departure appears to confirm our suspicions. On the last page of the manuscript (and the novel) Cova leaves a message for Clemente Silva instructing him to hand it over to the Colombian consul (which means at least one more reader) so that the information on the slavery issue contained therein might be made known to the government. The fact that the manuscript is also the artistic reflection of the spiritual and physical odyssey of the poet cannot but help his hitherto frustrated literary ambitions — if and when it falls into the hands of other readers.

Rivera, throughout the novel, skilfully fuses and confuses identities for artistic purposes (Cova/Silva, Cova/Ramírez), as I demonstrated earlier. He also does so with regard to himself (the author) and 'Rivera' of the Prologue, a fictionalization of the writer who has a novelesque role to play in the presentation of the authenticity and verisimilitude of the work (cf. the character 'Sábato' in *Abaddón el exterminador*). As I have been trying to suggest throughout this study, Cova is also a fictionalization of the author. What is even more interesting, as Ford too points out (*10*, p. 579), is that Cova himself, within the framework of his own manuscript, recreates a fictional character, 'Cova', who is also a literary figure. This 'Cova' who lives and fails and dies is the fictionalization of another Arturo Cova, the poet, who creates and stylizes a document which becomes the novel. That both Cova and 'Cova' are, when all is said and done, fictionalizations of the author Rivera, not to be confused with the editor/narrator 'Rivera' of the Prologue, is a tribute to the complex characterization and the subtly founded and skilfully developed narrative structure of the novel, which is composed of Arturo Cova's narrative, itself made up of the narratives of the other characters, Clemente Silva, Esteban Ramírez, Helí Mesa, Balbino Jácome, all of whose identities Cova adopts at some time in the novel.

The manuscript was purportedly written to Ramírez and left for Silva, who was to place it in the hands of the consul. The consul obviously sent it to the Minister who, we know from the Prologue passed it on to 'Rivera' who was to prepare it for publication. The number of readers has grown. It seems clear that the destined audience is larger than, and other than, that mentioned above. Given Cova's view of consuls, and government officials in general, confirmed by Clemente Silva's experiences throughout the novel, it is hardly likely that Cova would want his writing (however deep his social concern and patriotic feelings) to be directed solely to some nameless bureaucrat, some uncaring foreign mercenary in Manao. Whatever his alleged intention, one remembers the personal nature of Cova's manuscript, which is after all not merely the documentation of abuses, but also the artistic rendering of the most intimate secrets of his Romantic soul, with revealing insights into his tortured psyche. The manuscript may go to the consul, it may go then to the Minister, and it may be 'arranged' by 'Rivera', but there is without doubt yet another audience — those contemporaries mentioned in the letter fragment (7) who knew his ideals and dreams but who judged him and found him wanting; those who abandoned him in his time of failure. Let them think of what Cova might have been, could have been, if he had not been struck down by an implacable destiny. These words are not addressed to the alleged recipient, Ramírez, since they are taken from the letter accompanying the manuscript to be delivered by Clemente Silva to the consul, to whom Cova would hardly reveal such confidences. Since the letter was obviously passed to 'Rivera', who quotes the fragment published before the Prologue, the words are clearly directed to a wider audience, to posterity, to us. The implied reader has become the real reader, despite Cova's claims and the desire of 'Rivera' for non-involvement and distancing. What started out as a mere narrative, albeit the dramatized narrative of the unbalanced protagonist, purporting to be a patriotic exposé of social abuses, becomes the cornerstone of, if not, the novel itself.

Although Cova is the protagonist of, and the key to, the whole novel, and although all the characters live through him and depend on him for the telling of their stories, he is not ubiquitous. He has to rely, therefore, on the other characters (especially in the depiction of the slavery theme) for their narratives, which are then incorporated into the narrative (of Cova) as a whole. Each of the minor characters has a special role to play, chronologically and geographically, in the simplest terms, in the telling of the events that span almost two decades, within the eight months' duration of the novel. By portraying events not experienced by Cova, they add to the scope of the novel and Cova's vision of the world, thus extending and developing his character so that he may rise to the heights of social redeemer and even cosmic saviour by the end of the novel, prepared to avenge not only his own personal wrongs (Barrera) but those of his compatriots (El Cayeno, la Madona), and by extension all mankind in its struggle against evil, nature and destiny.

The first of these narrators is the old man Helí Mesa, whose story of the flight from Barrera's cruelty along with the other caucheros I have dealt with in some detail in Chapter 2. The telling of this story to Cova by a dramatized narrator has a positive effect on the action of the novel by highlighting the social evils for the first time, and thus anticipating Clemente Silva's long and important narrative on the key theme of exploitation. Helí Mesa's narrative is important also for the interpolation of the legend of the Indian princess Mapiripama, which contributes not only to the American folkloric element of the novel of the land, inextricably linked with the spiritual odyssey of Cova, but to the creation of the bewitched selva ambience, which is the cause and/or effect of Cova's growing madness. This technique of including the Indian legend is according to the theories of the Russian formalist, Tomashevsky, a 'free motif', and in the words of Roland Barthes an 'indice', since it serves to create an atmosphere of bewitchment (*2*, p. 273).[15] Benso, whose narrative division is firmly based on Green's theory of 'narradores dramatizados' and 'narradores disfrazados', tends, like Porras, to obscure simple divisions and levels by a mass of tables and numerals which contribute little to our deeper understanding of the novel. Helí Mesa is important as a narrator not only for himself and for his story of exploitation which prefigures Silva's, but also because of his role as an identity-vessel for Cova whose voice-assuming tendencies throughout the novel add a rich and ambiguous confusion of identities, which is not only aesthetically interesting but metaphysically satisfying, since it universalizes the individual problems of the various caucheros.

The most important narrator, apart from Cova, is Clemente Silva, the old rubber-worker guide, who also enters the novel in Part 2.

[15]Benso is referring here to the concept of 'free motif' (the unit added by the author which could be omitted without disturbing the causal-chronological course of events) as opposed to the 'bound motif' (the unit of the story which cannot be omitted without destroying the coherence of narrative). See Boris Tomashevsky's essay, 'Thematics', in *Russian Formalist Criticism: Four Essays* (Lincoln: University of Nebraska Press, 1965), pp. 61-95, esp. pp. 66-71. For a discussion of the 'indice' (an integrative unit which becomes significant only when seen in relation to a correlate on a higher level), see Roland Barthes, 'Introduction à l'analyse structurale des récits', *Communications* (1966), pp. 1-27, esp. pp. 8-9.

This dramatized narrator describes in detail events of many years in the jungle and the brutal treatment of the caucheros by the rubber magnates, including his own experiences, his search for his missing son, his meeting with the French scientist, the visitador, his escape, loss and sufferings in the jungle, before and after meeting Cova. His is the authentic voice of the selva, the true voice of protest speaking out against the personal social abuses (see Chapter 2 for details). This is all narrated in a way that Cova is not capable of, since the protagonist has not experienced these events first-hand. It is also significant that Cova sees in Silva not only the spiritual guide figure, but also the personification of the oppressed cauchero, with whom Cova wishes to identify — hence the aforementioned hymn of the cauchero scene which opens Part 3 (169-71), when Cova takes over the identity and the voice of Don Clemente to sing out the complaints against the jungle and life, which permit, even cause, the shattered dreams of rubber-workers and poets alike. Thus Cova, who has never known these particular experiences, comes under the influence of Silva's narrative and passes from 'observador' to 'agente'. I disagree with Green's argument (*14*, p. 105) that it is Clemente Silva who speaks here, with the florid and eloquent style of the poet. The reverse procedure is more likely, and more convincing. It seems to me, however, that it is much more effective to leave the passage in its more artistically pleasing ambiguous condition, which enriches the levels and the texture of the novel's narrative mode.

Within the framework of Silva's 'relato politemático' (to use Benso's phrase), which has its own position within the narrative frame of Cova's story, we hear third-hand, as it were, the mini-narrative of Balbino Jácome (157) and his experiences in the jungle, the terrible conditions which overwhelm the caucheros, the enormous debts handed down from father to son, and the crushing slavery which corrupts, dehumanizes and finally destroys men, women and children. Balbino Jácome's story reinforces Helí Mesa's, and complements that of Silva to whom he relates it; and it is one more integral part of the total narrative of Arturo Cova to whom it is relayed in turn by the intermediary Silva. All of their stories interlock just as their lives are implacably entwined by the selva, and their voices joined in a physical and spiritual protest against the evils which render them nameless, faceless and worthless in the eyes of a political and commercial system (Funes), symbol of a larger and wider system, Borges might say. Without forcing the analogy, I am suggesting that the narrative mode (like the structure of the novel) is a metaphor of the content, of the metaphysical vision which Rivera is presenting. This outlook is reinforced by the narrative of Esteban Ramírez, who, as we have seen, is not only the alter ego of Cova, and thus another confused identity, but because of the reversal of his name (Ramiro Estévanez), another face of himself as he was in the past, when, like Cova, he sought glory and happiness in life and marriage. Now, however, in the jungle, helpless, bitter, and blind, he narrates for Cova the history of the terrible massacre of the peons by Funes at San Fernando. In a chronological and structural sense, Ramírez has the important position of being the last narrator, whose story and narrative voice act as the catalyst which provokes, inspires, and persuades Cova to write his memoirs, which he claims to be doing only out of sympathy for his dejected friend, as a form of moral support and encouragement: 'No ambiciono otro fin que el de emocionar a Ramiro Estévanez con el breviario de mis aventuras, confesándole por escrito el curso de mis pasiones y defectos, a ver si aprende a apreciar en mí lo que en él regateó el destino, y logra estimularse para la acción, pues siempre ha sido provechosísima disciplina para el pusilánime hacer confrontaciones con el arriscado' (216-17). Purporting to copy down the events of San Fernando which Ramírez dictates to him, Cova writes an exposé of the rubber magnates' cruelties. Ramírez's story is only one of five, but Cova's decision to report the San Fernando atrocities as a social document gives the protagonist the initiative and the pretext for recording all the events which he had experienced and heard since leaving Bogotá − hence the justification for the inclusion of the other five narratives as integral parts of his story.

Each of the narrators tells his own story in his own way, in his own voice, reflecting his own vision of the jungle − and the world. Each story exists in and for itself, but, through the unifying voice and force of the principal narrator, the individual narratives are integrated into the whole by Cova's voice, and later by his manuscript. It is only by first separating, dismantling and extracting the various narratives that one hears the peculiarities of the individual voices. By restoring each narrative to its position in the framework of Cova's story, one begins to appreciate the integrity of the narrative mode within the temporal and spatial framework of the novel. Cova may be a dramatized narrator-agent who has a powerful influence on the action of the novel, but he is also an observer — not only of the jungle and events as he sees them, but as the others see them. In other words, Cova is not only the central figure around whom the others revolve, but also the key to the narrative mode, since he has to unify, organize and order the narrative parts of the the other narrators and present them to the reader. If these voices are modified and qualified by this filtering process, in aesthetic terms it is all for the better, since under Cova's treatment a group of different stories, which purportedly go to make up a mere document to encourage a friend and record social abuses, transcends these levels and reaches the wider audience long desired by Cova. The end result is a work of art, the novel *La vorágine*, which immortalizes the author behind all the characters, their voices, and their narratives.

I use intentionally the architectural terminology (framework, corner-stone, end-pieces, etc.) to describe the structure of *La vorágine*, whose aesthetic qualities stem from the fusion of *forma* and *fondo*, when the vehicle becomes the effect, and vice-versa. The cyclical nature of the novel, to which I have already alluded in the analogy with *Cien años de soledad*, becomes explicit with the termination of the manuscript, which then becomes the novel. This concentric nature of the vortex, as Seymour Menton has also pointed out (*17*, pp. 424-25), is a symbol not only of the jungle but of Cova's life and adventures therein, reflecting the never-ending internal spiralling of the whirlpool in all its forms (physical, psychological, metaphorical, literary).

Menton does well to stress this circular, cyclical narrative pattern of Cova's manuscript, which confirms my argument that if there is a fusion of content and form, and if form is in a sense a kind of metaphor of content, the structure of the narrative is more than just a framework or skeleton on which to hang the story. The structure, which thus becomes an integral part of the novel, is reflected in the narrative style or pattern of the poet-protagonist who absorbs the 'narración dispersa' of the 'narradores insertos' (Loveluck's phrase) into his own narrative to produce the unified manuscript, the fictional totality, which is the work of art, *La vorágine*.

7 Conclusion

In the Introduction, whilst keenly aware of the dangers of artificial divisions, I suggested that a fruitful method of examining a novel like *La vorágine*, whose complexity and profundity have been underestimated, would be to take it apart, to decompose it, in the nontechnical sense of the word, to display its various parts, its several levels or layers, and then re-examine the obvious dimensions whilst illuminating hitherto unappreciated aspects of this traditional novel. In this way, one can reconsider the value of *La vorágine* as a regionalist novel of the land or a harrowing document of social denunciation — two of the most relevant and obvious functions of the novel at the time of its publication in 1924. With the rapid progress in the field of psychology and the growing increase in scholarship on mythology, Freudian and Jungian interpretations of fiction help us to study more deeply the protagonist Arturo Cova and the other characters as types and archetypes, linked not only with modern man, but with figures of primitive societies and classical mythology. These new perspectives clearly help us to view the novel in more than regional and political terms, and raise it to the level of universal art, as I have been arguing throughout this work. When we can view Cova's odyssey not just in physical and geographical terms, but as a symbol of all men's search for absolute values, and of their failure to reach ideals in the eternal thirst for the infinite, for perfectibility, then *La vorágine* reveals itself as much more than an egocentric blast of propaganda.

Taking the novel apart is, of course, only the first stage of the analytical process, and a mere pretext to see better the totality of the work of art. Ever mindful of Plato's admonition to Socrates and his followers not to fragment irreparably the object of our scrutiny for fear of missing the meaning and the significance of the whole, I have throughout linked the parts, being careful to put them together again in a meaningful work of reconstruction. Another image to describe the critical process which I have been using may be a strand of multi-coloured, multi-textured wool, made up of various threads, each of which can be removed from the strand and examined and admired for and by itself. Interesting and fascinating as it is, the individual thread becomes more interesting and attractive when intertwined and tangled again with the other threads to form the fibre of the whole strand, more solid, more compact, more complex, more rich, more textured, and more colourful in its totality. This is what I mean by decomposing or deconstructing the novel, and this is my justification for the critical approach adopted in this study. It is clear, of course, that this approach is but a pretext or a device to demonstrate the varied richness of the complete work, and is but an intermediate stage in the process towards an ideal reading of the novel — that is, viewing it as a totality whose interdependent and mutually supporting strata, threads, or parts (to continue the analogies suggested throughout) fuse to form the complete work of art.

Whilst in the study of the novel I have had cause to refer to the life of the author, I have striven to avoid identifying wholly Fiction and Biography, the protagonist Arturo Cova with his creator José Eustasio Rivera. However, he cannot, as Sartre would wish, be totally isolated from his fictional creation. Behind every literary figure stands an author. If I have drawn some parallels between the life of Rivera and the character portrayed in the novel, it is not to suggest that *La vorágine* is an autobiographical novel, but merely to show, in passing, that Cova, as complex a figure as one will find in modern fiction, manifests, not surprisingly, some of the philosophical, political and aesthetic concerns of his creator.

La vorágine will survive not because it is a reflection of the life of José Eustasio Rivera, but because it is an authentic work of fiction containing a fascinating protagonist, portrayed in a convincing and artistic manner. It will, of course, be a work of art only if the form used corresponds to the content described. It is for this reason that I have spent some time replying to the charges of formlessness and lack of unity which have been levelled against the novel over the years. Thus *La vorágine* must surely, once and for all, be considered a universal work of art, transcending the personal and regional dimensions, important as the novel may be on those planes. But as Jean Franco felicitiously expressed it: 'The justification of the novel must be on the grounds of the total vision of human experience that it presents . . .' (*11*, p. 110). As in all universally acclaimed works of literature, *La vorágine* represents a perfect synthesis of metaphysics and aesthetics.

Bibliographical Note

1. Añez, Jorge, *De 'La vorágine' a 'Doña Bárbara'*. Bogotá: Impresión del Departamento, 1944. Suggests obvious debts of Gallegos' novel to *La vorágine*.

2. Benso, Silvia, '*La vorágine*: una novela de relatos', *Thesaurus*, 30 (1975), 271-90. Uninspired structural study of the novel, based on *14*.

3. Bull, William E., 'Nature and Anthropomorphism in *La vorágine*', *Romanic Review*, 39 (1948), 307-18. Quite interesting early study of the connection between the selva and the psychological evolution of the protagonist.

4. Callan, Richard J., 'The Archetype of Psychic Renewal in *La vorágine*', *Hispania* (U.S.A.), 54 (1971), 470-76. Sophisticated, imaginative, and truly original interpretation (Jungian) of the novel.

5. — —., '*La vorágine*: A Touchstone of Character', *Romance Notes*, 3 (1961-62), 13-16. Slight piece on the jungle's influence on the characters.

6. Curcio Altamar, Antonio., 'La novela terrígena', in his *Evolución de la novela en Colombia* (Bogotá: Instituto Colombiano de Cultura, 1975), pp. 175-85. Standard material on *La vorágine* as a novel of the land.

7. Charria Tobar, Ricardo, *José Eustasio Rivera en la intimidad*. Bogotá: Editorial Tercer Mundo, 1963. Gossipy and self-serving collection of short light pieces of no literary value.

8. Eyzaguirre, Luis B., 'Arturo Cova; héroe patológico', in his *El héroe en la novela hispanoamericana del siglo XX* (Santiago de Chile: Editorial Universitaria, 1973), pp. 46-65. Occasional insightful comments on Cova as the Romantic hero with pathological weaknesses.

9. — —., 'Patología en *La vorágine* de José Eustasio Rivera', *Hispania* (U.S.A.), 56 (1973), 81-90. Repeat of *8*.

10. Ford, Richard, 'El marco narrativo de *La vorágine*', *Revista Iberoamericana*, 42, nos 96-97 (1976), 573-80. Very useful and provocative article on the narrative structure, which makes good points and asks intelligent questions about the structure, arrangement, and readers.

11. Franco, Jean, 'Image and Experience in *La vorágine*', *Bulletin of Hispanic Studies*, 41 (1964), 101-10. Interesting and illuminating article which shows *La vorágine* and its protagonist to be in the Romantic tradition.

12. Gómez Restrepo, Antonio, 'José Eustasio Rivera', in *Crítica literaria* (Bogotá: Editorial Minerva, 1935), pp. 185-97. Significantly, deals only with the poetry of *Tierra de promisión*, given his negative view of *La vorágine*.

13. González, Alfonso, 'Elementos hispánicos y clásicos en la caracterización de *La vorágine*', *Cuadernos Americanos*, 200 (1975), 248-54. Routine comparisons with Don Quijote, Don Juan, etc.

14. Green, Joan R., 'La estructura del narrador y el modo narrativo de *La vorágine*', *Cuadernos Hispanoamericanos*, 69 (1967), 101-07. One of the earliest and best treatments of the narrative mode and voices.

15. Herrera Molina, Luis Carlos. *José Eustasio Rivera: poeta de promisión*.

Bogotá: Instituto Caro y Cuervo, 1968. Useful general study of the man and the artist, his symbols, metaphors, and language.

16. Loveluck, Juan, 'Prólogo' to *La vorágine*. Caracas: Biblioteca Ayacucho, 1976, pp. ix-xliii. Bitty but useful introductory potted study of Rivera's life and work, covering various aspects of the novel.

17. Menton, Seymour, '*La vorágine*: Circling the Triangle', *Hispania* (U.S.A.), 59 (1976), 418-34. Fascinating and illuminating Christian interpretation of the novel based on Dante's *Divine Comedy*.

18. Morales, Leónidas. '*La vorágine*: un viaje al país de los muertos', *Anales de la Universidad de Chile*, 123 (1965), 148-70. Good early mythological interpretation of the novel based on Virgil's *Aeneid*.

19. Neale-Silva, Eduardo, *Estudios sobre José Eustasio Rivera: el arte poético*. New York: Hispanic Institute, 1951. Solid study of the verses of *Tierra de promisión*.

20. — —, 'The Factual Bases of *La vorágine*', *PMLA*, 54 (1939), 316-31. Absolutely vital for the literary detective who wants to have all the facts (historical, geographical, botanical, folkloric, anthropological, etc.) about the composition of the novel.

21. — —, *Horizonte humano: vida de José Eustasio Rivera*. Mexico City: Fondo de Cultura Económica, 1960. The only real biography of Rivera, diligently researched, admirably detailed and comprehensive, an invaluable guide to the life and works of Rivera.

22. Olivera, Otto, 'El romanticismo de José Eustasio Rivera', *Revista Iberoamericana*, 36 (1953), 41-61. Predictable reading of the poetry, novel and life of Rivera.

23. Osuna, Rafael, 'Anagnorisis en *La vorágine*, de Rivera', *Revista de Indias*, 27 (1967), 461-68. Mildly useful but slight study of the various surprise meetings and changed identities in the novel.

24. Perera, Hilda, *Aspectos de 'La vorágine'*. Santiago de Cuba: Manigua, 1956. Trivial, uninteresting and singularly unhelpful general remarks.

25. Pope, Randolph D., '*La vorágine*: Autobiografía de un intelectual', in *The Analysis of Literary Texts: Current Trends in Methodology*, Third and Fourth York College Colloquia, ed. Randolph D. Pope (Ypsilanti, Michigan: Bilingual Press, 1980), pp. 256-67. Fresh and interesting look at Cova as an intellectual and his place in a hostile society.

26. Porras Collante, Ernesto, 'Hacia una interpretación estructural de *La vorágine*', *Thesaurus*, 23 (1968), 241-79. Disappointing and pretentiously presented examination of the structure of the novel.

27. Ramos, Oscar Gerardo, 'Clemente Silva, héroe de *La vorágine*', *Boletín Cultural y Bibliográfico* (Bogotá), 10 (1968), 568-82. Modest attempt to promote Clemente Silva, because of his special role in the jungle, to the postion of hero.

28. Spell, Jefferson Rea, 'The Secrets of the *Selvas* of Colombia Unfolded by José Eustacio [sic] Rivera', in his *Contemporary Spanish American Fiction* (Chapel Hill: University of North Carolina Press, 1944), pp. 179-90. Typically limited discussion of the novel from the point of view of plot, characterization, and themes, by a pioneer critic of twentieth-century Latin-American fiction.

29. Torres, Mauro, '*La vorágine*, catarsis y síntesis de un tormento psíquico', in his *Dialéctica de los sueños* (Bogotá: Ediciones de la Universidad Libre de Colombia, 1962), pp. 175-214. An interesting and truly psychiatric (as

opposed to psychological) analysis of the unbalanced protagonist.

30. Valbuena-Briones, A., 'El arte de José Eustasio Rivera', *Thesaurus*, 17 (1962), 129-39. Thin summary of the life and works of Rivera.

31. Valente, José Angel, 'La naturaleza y el hombre en *La vorágine* de José Eustasio Rivera', *Cuadernos Hispanoamericanos*, 67 (1955), 102-08. Usual treatment of man and the jungle.

32. Viñas, David, '*La vorágine*: crisis, populismo y mirada', *Hispamérica*, 3, no. 8 (1974), 3-21. Dense and disappointing study of the possible motivation and destination of the protagonist.

33. Williamson, Rodney, '*La vorágine* y sus críticos: una revaloración', *Ottawa Hispánica*, no. 2 (1980), 1-32. A very useful summary of the most recent critical perspectives, especially of Callan (*4*, Jungian) and Menton (*17*, Christian).

CRITICAL GUIDES TO SPANISH TEXTS

Edited by
J.E. Varey and A.D. Deyermond